Why not me?

Henry D. Bartak

Why not me?
Copyright © 2019 by Henry D. Bartak

All rights reserved. No part of this publication may be reproduced, distributed, or transmitted in any form or by any means, including photocopying, recording, or other electronic or mechanical methods, without the prior written permission of the author, except in the case of brief quotations embodied in critical reviews and certain other non-commercial uses permitted by copyright law.

Tellwell Talent
www.tellwell.ca

ISBN
978-0-2288-1341-5 (Paperback)

Front dedication

I wrote this story so my son knows my side of his family story. So we may become Father and Son like I always wanted us to be. And to my Mother, and Narcis who both watch over me. My Father and his wonderful wife, Shirley who accepted me after so many years apart. My Brothers, Tomas, Milan for setting the standards that I looked up for. Carmen, my long lost sister how much I wish to be the older brother for. Deanna, may we meet once again. My first love and strongest friend I ever had. Jacquie Cassie and how much you changed my life, I thank you! Aron Apeldorn for my proof reads and honesty truly helped me to finish my story. To everyone who stood by me, gave me opportunities and believed in me. I grew strength from you, and most of all I figured out who I am. And that I am loved. God bless you all!

Chapter 1 – The Old Country

Prague 04/12/1968

It's a dry, cold, breezy day on the streets of Prague. Inside a small café, burnt toast and fresh coffee lingers in the air. As lunch rush finishes, a beautiful young waitress with green eyes and long curly red hair that is tied up in the back leans over the counter to grab someone's dirty dishes and gives the counter a wipe.

"Rosa! Pick up!" is heard from across the room. Dennis, a tall, handsome, slender man with dark hair, blue eyes and a rough, chiselled look removes his cook's hat and wipes the sweat from his forehead with a towel. He puts the towel into his belt and adjusts his apron.

"Rosa!" he calls out again. He peers past the food tickets and through the counter window that separates the kitchen from the dining area. He stares for a moment at Rosa as she finishes wiping the counter. He is in a trance.

"I am coming, Dennis," Rosa calls back.

The café is small and cozy on this cold winter's day. A fire burns in the wood stove, and half a dozen customers are eating and talking.

One of the regular customers gets up from his table and crouches by the fire. He picks up a small log from the pile and puts it gently on the fire. Sparks shoot up with a puff of smoke and he sits back down feeling good that he has tended the chore of his afternoon.

A few people are having coffee at the front counter and discussing the upcoming policies of the near future. With the local Czechoslovakian government leaning more towards imperialistic ideas, Russia is growing impatient. The local citizens are afraid of the potential invasion of the Russian military and the rise of communism. Tensions are escalating and in the air is thick with conversations about what might happen.

A short, older, potbellied, balding gentleman wearing a long, heavy-collared jacket walks in the front door and with him comes a blast of cold air. He removes his unusually small hat and flips his cigarette out to the road. He throws his hat and jacket onto the counter and lights another cigarette. Stepping behind the counter and looking into the kitchen he says, "Dennis! How are you?" Mr. Lubomir, a solid business man and owner of the cafe, spent five years in the Czech Army and is always proud to tell stories for hours.

"Ahoy! I am well Mr. Lubomir," replies Dennis as he chops bread into croutons. He dumps them into a big silver mixing bowl. "Any news that is good, sir?" he says.

Mr. Lubomir pours himself a coffee, and walks over to the cash register and takes a sip. He grabs the day's receipts and cash from the register.

"More pressure from the city. They are raising the taxes and adding additional fees to our business in order to compensate for political parties. I must get to the bank before they close today."

He starts organizing the receipts on the counter. "The good news is our new waitress, Rosa, is doing a terrific job and she's not bad to look at, too, don't you agree, Dennis? Dennis?"

He turns his head around to see Dennis still with his head through the counter window full of food tickets. "Let's make her feel welcome and hopefully she sticks around for a while, OK Dennis?"

Dennis wipes his forehead, nods and goes back to prepping food. Mr. Lubomir gathers his receipts, puts his jacket and small hat on, and leaves the store for the bank.

08/20/1968

It's a hot, sunny afternoon at the café. Rosa is at the register giving change to a customer.

"Have a nice day, Peter," she tells the tall, clean-shaven middle aged man as he walks out the door.

"Rosa, pick up!" calls Dennis.

Rosa picks up the meals and their eyes meet through the window. She smiles. Dennis is obviously madly in love with her. His eyes are wide and vulnerable, like a puppy's.

"Rosa will you come over tonight?" he asks, poking his head through the window. "I have a fine bottle of wine? I will make a tasty meal for dinner, meat and dumplings. What you say?"

She sets her soft palm on the side of his face and smiles. "You know I have plans with my husband and sons tonight. We will get together on Thursday night, okay?"

She wipes the sweat off his forehead then he grabs her hand, pulls her a bit closer and whispers, "I love you, Rosa. Please, I need to see you."

He tries to kiss her but he can't fit through the window at the counter. She shakes her head and her smile turns into a half smile. Looking him in the eyes, she says, "You know I feel the same but we must be patient. I cannot hurt my family more than I have. If you love me like you say, you will respect me. Trust me. We will be together my love." She kisses him.

Chapter 2 – A Few Hours Earlier

Meanwhile, in a high school woodworking class across town, a tall, skinny, freckled young man about 15 years old with long, curly, blazing red hair flowing to his shoulders is cutting pieces of wood on a table saw.

"Milan! You never going to finish your cabinet in time if you keep fussing over the measurements," says Mr. Dominic Sipla, the shop teacher. He is a tall, older gentleman who wears a gray suit and tie that is covered in sawdust and shavings.

"I will finish, sir. I will stay late to make sure, sir. If it's OK?" Milan replies while picking up his cut pieces.

The instructor shouts back over the sound of class working away, "I think it is alright, Milan. But, I expect high quality from you with all the extra time you spend here."

Milan smiles and puts his head down to the piece of wood and continues to measure. His love and passion for cabinetry is obvious to his teacher and fellow classmates. He puts a piece of cut lumber through the planer and catches it on the other end. He always has four to six projects going at the same time: a lounge chair for his father, a table for his instructor, a stool for another teacher so his wife can reach things in the kitchen, a mirror for a cute girl in his literature class and, of course, his own projects. He's building a chess table so he and his brother can play.

A tall, skinny 13-year-old boy with long dark hair past his shoulders walks up to Milan. "Hey brother!" Tomas says, slapping Milan on the back just as he is hammering a nail. Milan screams in pain as he misses the nail and pounds his thumb.

"Aaaaahhhhoch!" he screams.

Realizing what just happened Tomas jumps back in surprise. "I been waiting for you—are you coming?" he asks Milan.

"Cmon! That fucking hurts! Pay attention! I'm going to lose my nail now!" He wraps his thumb with his shirt and takes a breather before starting again. "Sorry, I got busy with this, I can't make it bro, sorry. I need to stay and finish in order to achieve my final grade." Milan wraps up his thumb with some black tape and continues to hammer. "I will catch up with you later," he says, putting a piece of wood on the table saw.

"OK Milan, I will see you later at home. Sorry for your thumb," Tomas says. He starts to walk away but stops, turns around looking back at Milan.

Milan flips the switch and the RPMs of the blade are deafening.

"Hey! Milan! Brother! Milan!" he shouts till he gets his brother's attention. Milan switches the table saw off, and the blade quickly slows down. "What you think of Mom and Dad? They have not been themselves for quite some time now. You think Dad is seeing someone else?"

Milan looks up and shrugs; he doesn't know what to say to his younger brother. He doesn't believe himself when he says, "I am sure it is nothing, no I don't think he is. Now go! I need to finish." He flips the switch and continues cutting the wood.

--

Rosa walks out the front door of the café after her shift. She has about twelve blocks to walk home. Along the way she stops into the neighbourhood Pivovar Pub, where just about every person is smoking a cigarette. She makes her way through the blue cloud of haze to a tall, gorgeous brunette with a green knee-high skirt and dark stockings on her long legs. She's wearing blue earrings and a necklace that matches her eyes. She's chatting with a young blonde man with a beard and mustache who is smoking a cigarette.

"Hello gorgeous!" Rosa says, wrapping her arms around the young lady and giving her a kiss on the cheek. Sasha is a short, well-proportioned woman with a beauty mark right on the front tip of her nose.

"Hi Rosa, beer?" asks the Jose the bartender, a good looking, tanned, middle-aged man from Spain.

"Yes, thank you, Jose," she replies then turns to Sasha. "Hi Sasha," she whispers into her ear, trying not to be too much of a distraction for the flirty couple.

"Hi! My favourite person in the Czechoslovakian territory," Sasha says as she turns around and gives Rosa a hug and kiss on the cheek. "I want to introduce my new friend, Tony, he is an engineer!" Sasha tells her as she turns back around to him and steps aside so they can shake hands. Rosa steps forward and is in awe of his charm.

"Hello, Rosa. I have heard a lot about you this last hour," says Tony.

"Hello, I can't say the same unfortunately. This is a surprise to me." Rosa is not sure what to say, but adds, "But, I am glad for my best friend. You sure are a handsome fella." She scans him up one side and down the other.

Half a dozen beers and a couple of hours later, the three are laughing and talking and smoking.

"Oh! It's getting late, Sasha. I must be getting home. Karl will be home soon. It's been great to meet you, Tony," Rosa says, shaking his hand. Rosa leans over to Sasha's ear and whispers. They laugh and give each other a hug and kiss.

Rosa staggers out of the pub. It's hot and dry outside compared to the cool pub. But the air is fresh as she lifts her head back and closes her eyes. She inhales and exhales slowly and deeply. She makes her way down the street and lights a cigarette. Her brain is fuzzy in the fresh air, and oh the cigarette is like icing on the cake. The sun is slowly setting and it's a beautiful evening, she thinks.

Meanwhile at City Hall, Tomas and a dozen of his friends from school are amongst a huge crowd gathering in the streets. Hundreds of people are protesting against the Russian influences and the Warsaw Pact. People are scared of the reprisals and angry at their local government. The crowd is growing larger by the minute. People are restless and scared, mad and desperate. Signs with anti-Russian messages are held high and protesters wave Czech flags patriotically. The crowd is yelling and trying to get their point across to anyone who is inside the building. Hopefully, the mayor is there. With a bang, jets fly ever so fast overhead. The protesters throw rocks and sticks and bottles at the police.

The Czech police and military personnel are gathering in an offensive line. Sirens blare through the streets. The odd smoke grenade is tossed into the mob, as the police try to thin the crowd out. The smoke is thick and huge amounts come from such a small cylinder.

"Get out of here, Tomas! It's going to get worse!" a short, thin, bearded man named Hendry says.

"Yes! We all need to. It is not safe here anymore! I need to get home," Tomas replies as he picks up an old woman who had fallen.

People are now restless and desperate, there's smoke everywhere, and a stampede is beginning. Arms and hands reach out from the smoke and grab the bearded man.

"RUN TOMAS!! They have me! HELP ME!" he yells out.

Tomas grabs a policeman and chokes him till he releases his grip on the bearded man. Just as they start to run, more arms and hands reach out and grab them both. Tomas is able to get free and flees without looking back. Screams and gun shots are more intense and louder. He continues to run as fast as he can, jumping over backyard fences and through bushes. He ends up about eight blocks away and right on the edge of a park.

He hides behind a tree, stooped over to catch his breath. The sirens blare in the distance. People are screaming and yelling for help. Smoke is everywhere and Tomas tries in vain to wipe the sting from his eyes. His vision is blurry and his nose burns. Other people are running away with police and military personnel in pursuit. He has to get home and tell everyone! They must run for their lives.

POP POP POP!!! rings out. Shots are being fired. He knows the Russian invasion is coming. More Russian fighter jets soar through the skies, breaking the sound barrier. Tanks roll through the streets across from him. People are getting arrested and beaten up—some are shot right before his eyes. It is total chaos.

He thinks of his mother and father, hoping they are home already. He figures Milan will be OK because he's a tough, stubborn guy. Tomas takes cover in the alleys on his way home, praying to be back before sundown. Turning down a street, Tomas bumps into two Czech police officers who are arresting a young boy. The boy's face is badly beaten.

"Stop!" yells one of the police officers at Tomas.

Tomas knows if he stops his face will be badly beaten as well, so he runs as fast as he can the other way until he realizes they never even bothered with him.

Rosa walks along, enjoying her buzz from the few beers. She is heavy in thought about her life and how she is in love with another man. As she looks at the cracks in the sidewalk, thoughts of her family and what she should do about her new love distract her. Sounds of chaos get louder and clearer as she gets closer to downtown. One by one people start running by her. "RUN!" they yell.

But she has to get home and she has to go this way! Rosa is trembling with the thoughts of getting arrested. She has heard many stories of friends who were arrested, beaten and tortured. She cautiously continues on when all of a sudden the ground trembles beneath her and the windows and walls of the buildings shake. *Earthquake?* she wonders. The sounds are louder and more thunderous. Then she hears the squeal of steel.

Tanks.

She darts into an alley. More people are running away from the direction she has to go. She's bumped and jostled trying to push her way through crowded streets. She falls hard onto her back and hits her head on the ground. She's dazed, her vision blurred. Someone grabs her by the hair and pulls her to her feet.

"Run! Run!!" she hears but can't see anyone in front of her. *Which way?* she wonders, but is quickly pulled and she runs. Her sight starts to come back but her head aches. A big bump is bleeding and sweat runs down her back. Her shirt is stained red.

There! She sees a break in the crowd and quickens her stride. She bumps her way through—only two more blocks to the bridge and home is near! She scrambles to get through but is going against the flow. Now, the Russian military are marching toward her, hurling gas canisters. She has no choice. There's no way to go around. She fights her way through people screaming and yelling.

"I must get home! I must get my boys!" she yells out, hoping for someone to help her. No one hears her cries. Everyone is doing the exact same thing. Her clothing is getting ripped as she desperately fights the mob. Finally, she breaks through the last line of people and she is in the open. Now she's facing the armed military personnel who are marching towards her. Buildings on both sides, protesters behind her, she runs towards the shoe shop on the left but the door is locked. She tries the neighbouring store—nothing.

"Halt!!" yells a Russian solider who is holding a rifle. He's backed up by two more soldiers who are holding rifles to her head.

Tomas crashes through the door at home, huffing and puffing and sweating.

"Tomas, I am so glad to see you!" his father says. "Where is your brother?" Karl is taller than his two sons but not by much. An educated, stern but fair man, he wants his boys to be great.

"Father, you have no idea how bad it is. The military is here!" Tomas replies, heading to the kitchen for water. "Last I saw Milan was in class. Where is Mother?"

Karl is now concerned, but he's prepared. "I was expecting her a couple hours ago, I am worried. I heard they are taking people, arresting innocent civilians," he says.

They run through the house looking to see if mother was hiding somewhere and also to pack their belongings—whatever they can carry and bring with them across the border.

"We must wait for them," Karl says. "I have a safe place for us to go, then we can make a run to the Austrian border. Your mother and I have planned for this, we will be safe there. I know someone who can help us. We will go to Canada and start a new life!"

Karl and Tomas are gathering supplies and piling them by the front door. At that moment the front door flies open and Milan is there, gasping for air. "They are coming!" he yells. "We have to leave now! Where is Mother?" As he scans the home he can't see her.

"She has not come home yet, we are worried about her," Karl says, concern written on his face.

Tomas is upstairs gathering what he thought they would need. Milan scrambles through the house looking from window to window, desperately praying to see his mother coming. Karl loads the car and hurries the boys out the door. He has a bad gut feeling that she may have been arrested. *May Christ save us*, he says to himself.

They drive down a dirt road for three hours, crossing damaged bridges barely safe enough to drive over. The mountains are just ahead. Karl reassures his sons as best he can, even though he fears the worst.

"Your mother and I discussed this scenario and she knows we will meet her at the cabin," Karl says from the driver's seat. "We said if anything was ever to happen to either of us then the other should take you two boys to the cabin. There, we wait as long as we can, otherwise then we must do whatever we must after that."

"She would have had to go through them in order to get home, I saw it! There is no way she could have made it," says Tomas as he looks out the window, crying. He is searching out the window to see if he can spot her. Milan is in the front seat and is angry that they left without her. He remains quiet for a while. They drive into the night. It's still quite hot even at night. They are thirsty and only eat a little bit of bread to get by. They should be at the cabin soon.

All seems well when they arrive and they figure no one has made it out here so far. Branches are strewn across the driveway as it has been a couple of years since Karl and Rosa came for a "weekend getaway." The cabin was their retirement plan—pay it off and move to the country. It was an older hunter's cabin that Karl bought from the son of his best friend. It needed some work and every time they came up, they worked on something new. But, bills piled up and tension around travelling prevented them from coming. Karl and Rosa kept paying on their home in the country. One day they figured there would be peace and happier days.

Two Russian guards drag Rosa into a cell and slam the door behind her. She has fallen onto the dirt floor that's wet with urine, puke and blood. She is in great pain. There are a dozen other women in the cell and none of them are over thirty. All are beat up pretty badly. She sits on the floor with the others. She sees other cells in the room and each are filled with men, women and children.

"They want information on your husbands, where they work and who they are friends with," one of the women in the cell sitting on the bench says. Her arm is in a sling and she has two black eyes. "They are torturous bastards and they want the good looking young girls separate from the rest."

"You know why," another person says from the floor.

Two Russian soldiers pace the hallway by the cells. Rosa is exhausted and closes her eyes. She is crouched on the floor when the cell door opens. A policeman enters with three women by the arms and push them down the hall through a doorway. They seem to also be wives, mothers of other civilian families that the authorities are looking for. Rosa is exhausted and doesn't have the energy to resist. The women are marched into separate rooms and thrown to the floor. There's only a light bulb in the ceiling as the big sliding bar lock clanks shut.

Rosa curls in a ball on the floor and covers her ears but she can't help but hear the screams a few rooms down. Crying and scared, she passes out. She is awoken by loud screams and has no idea how long she's been out. She crouches in the corner in a somewhat dry spot away from the rest of the women.

It seems like hours go by when someone finally comes to her cell. The door opens and a guard puts a tray of food and a cup of water on the floor. He shuts the heavy door behind him. She wishes she didn't have to, but she is brutally hungry. And she is so very thirsty. It's some cold meat—probably horse—and a stale bun with a pickle but she doesn't care at this point. It could be her last meal. She pours the last drop from the cup to her lips and feels the coolness of the water drop gently on her tongue.

After a few minutes, she has severe cramps and starts feeling nausea and weakness. She curls back on the damp, cold floor, shivering.

A few hours later, a guard with a pitcher of water walks in. He tells Rosa to wash herself and instead she drinks all the water because she is so thirsty.

"You must be looking better quickly, the captain will be back shortly," he says over and over. He leaves when the pitcher is done. A few minutes later he is back, this time with a dress and shoes.

"Put this on, now!" He hands her a white wedding dress and shoes. There is blood all over the dress and one shoe is size 5 and the other a 6. Trembling, she fumbles the dress and shoes on. Just as she buttons the last breast button, the door swings open. Two guards spray perfume on her and tell her to brush her hair.

"The captains are waiting!" one of the tall Russian guards yells at Rosa. They grab her and force her to walk down the hallway.

Two weeks go by and Karl and the boys are still at the cabin waiting and hoping and starving. But they can't give up on their mother. Word gets around through on the radio that the city is under control by the Russian military. Slowly, groups of soldiers are inspecting every farm house and cabin that are close to Prague. People are escaping over the borders, and citizens are getting caught and sent back. Trying to save on any power to the radio, they periodically listen to the updates of the invasion. They fear they'll never see Rosa again. Milan is constantly angered and in search of news about her. Tomas is quiet and keeps to himself or close to his father. Karl is barely holding himself together but he can't show his boys, so he keeps a constant straightforward look.

"We are running out of food, I think we should make our way, boys," Karl says in a low, discerning tone. He looks at Milan who is the oldest, "Your mother will find us, we have talked about it. You boys must trust me, we must leave now!" he says grabbing Milan by the shoulders.

Tomas stands up and looks out the window. "Someone is coming!" he yells.

"Be quiet! What do you see?" Milan says as he crowds by the only window. They can see down the long driveway to the gate, and there is a chain across the lane.

"It looks like someone is hurt, they barely can walk. Should we help?" Tomas says.

The verdant driveway is lined with trees and berry-stuffed bushes. It's hard to see the face of the limping person, who is obviously in distress. The driveway winds down and they lose sight for a few minutes, but coming through one of the bends, the sight is clean.

"No, it could be a trap. Just wait and be quiet. Don't do anything," Karl tells his sons. He is anxious to find out himself.

The figure is limping on one shoe, and raises their arm.

"I think someone is in trouble," Tomas says. Then the figure comes crashing down; their legs gave out from under them. Karl, Tomas and Milan run out of the house towards the fallen figure.

"It's Mommy!" Tomas yells. Before anyone else has the chance to look he is already running down the driveway.

Tomas sees the bruises on her face and arms and struggles to help her to her feet.

"MOM! I have you, its Tomas. You are ok, Mom!" he says.

They all help carry Rosa into the cabin. They set her on the bed and bring her water. Tomas wets a towel and wipes the dried blood and mud from his mother's face. This reveals deep bruises; she is in rough shape. Her feet are swollen and have cuts all over from walking for seven days in the dry hot summer. Judging by her wrists, she was bound with chains and it's the same on her ankles. There are big bruises and burn marks all over her body.

"I was beaten," she says weakly. "I was chained up and not fed for days while in custody. I must have passed out for 72 hours but it's all a blank—I can recall very little of what happened since I last saw you." She would hardly say a word to anyone, and she was different now.

"You can see it in her eyes, something terrible happened to our mother," Milan tells Tomas.

"We must leave still, even more now," Karl says.

They all agree that they must leave for the border right away. They make a bed-like comfy place in the trunk, figuring if they got stopped it would be impossible to explain Rosa's condition. So, she lies in comfort in the trunk. They will stop to check on her every few miles of the 150-mile journey to the train that will take them to Austria. They load the car with what's left of their supplies and Mom is comfy. She is in and out of consciousness and hanging in there. Karl and the boys look back at the cabin, they reminisce of years gone by. Karl pops the clutch and away they go. CANADA!

A few months go by, and the whole family is finally in Canada. After a couple of weeks of bureaucratic red tape and the kids being held in a foster home, they are given keys to their apartment. They're in Scarborough, Ontario, and it's cold!

"Close the door, Tomas! Where have you been?" yells Milan from the table in the living room.

"We will have our first Christmas here, in Canada! Scarborough, Ontario, Canada!" shouts Tomas back. "I was at a mall looking for your present but it is hard to communicate. I don't know how to speak English. It's hard in the new school, too." He looks at Milan and smiles. "But we are free! We are Canadians! We will learn English!" he says.

He looks at Rosa, who is wearing a beautiful blue flowered dress and has her red hair curly and long. She is motionless and quiet sitting at the edge of the table. Tomas has had a cough for a month now and Rose never saw a doctor when she arrived in Canada. They been too busy escaping and travelling and making a new home. They were on a list but with the influx of refugees into the area, there was a shortage in services.

The small apartment has two small bedrooms. Milan has one and Rosa and Karl the other. They hung a sheet up dividing the living room so Tomas has a room as well. A table with five chairs sits on the other side of the sheet where they eat their meals. Karl got a job as a cleaner in a school. It was hard not knowing the language but they managed just like others who escaped Czechoslovakia and made their way to North America. Milan smiles and puts the plates on the table prior to dinner.

"Hey Brother, you notice anything out of the ordinary with Mom?" Tomas asks.

"Like what?" Milan replies.

"She is more quiet and withdrawn. I know they must have done unimaginable things to her. I hope she will be OK?" Tomas replies.

"She will be fine, Brother, have no worry. I will keep my eyes open to her more often. OK?" Milan asks.

Through the next few months Rosa becomes more alert and talkative. She is still blank on the two weeks of her incarceration and she is very combative and questioning. At one moment, she is nice and pleasant, then flip a switch and she is telling false stories and accusing Karl of outrageous things. And the boys get their fair share of accusations as well. Miscommunication and mass confusion escalates because Karl is constantly scratching his head trying to reason with his wife. She makes stories up and whether they're true or false, no one knows.

The family is having a hard, hard time dealing with everything. Milan and Tomas can not speak English yet and only have each other to look out for. Now they must be challenged by their mother and her abnormal behaviour. Yet, she is out at all hours of the day and staying awake through the night. Constantly angry and depressed, she battles endlessly with herself. The doctors prescribe valium and a counsellor to speak with but it's obvious that the time she spent with the authorities in Prague really did some physiological damage. After sixteen months, Rosa asks for a divorce. Her family thinks she is having a relationship with someone else. Tomas and Milan were very confused and in disbelief of their family situation and wished they knew how to help her. The end of Karl and Rosa's relationship came after March 1969.

A few weeks earlier, Rosa had been working part time at a café in downtown Scarborough, when the front door opens. In comes a tall, handsome fella with a chiselled look who she recognizes immediately—it's Dennis from back home. They look at each other and embrace like it was only yesterday since they had last seen each other. They held each other tight; it was lost love found. By June, Rosa and Dennis were engaged.

The first year was healing for Rose. She felt rescued and loved like she had lost herself so long ago. By February 1970, I was born in Scarborough, Ontario. Dennis and Rose were in the stars beyond happy with their new family. Tomas and Milan were dealing with their experience in their own way, both concentrating on the new school and friends, as well as understanding a new culture and language. As long as their mother was safe and happy, they were fine. They had a lot on their plate plus Karl insisted they do well in school.

I wouldn't meet them until I turned two years old. My mother contacted Tomas and asked him to watch me for the afternoon. He hesitated for a bit, but agreed only because the sound of his mother's voice was like a frightened little girl's; it was difficult to listen to. She told him things were not well at home. She tells him a story so hard to believe, that he is shaken up.

My father's feelings for Rosa were strong and he wanted to propose to her. As the story goes, one weekend late in June, Tomas and Milan helped their mother move her things out of one man's home and into another. Tomas and Milan were devastated by their mother's actions and were totally surprised by it all. What could anyone do? She was in love with another man and pregnant with his child. They would not marry but lived with each other just across town from her boys.

Dennis was a good distraction for Rosa for a while. But, she continued to behave oddly. Her boys were giving her their time when it was convenient, of course for them this was hard enough to fit in with the new country they are conforming to. It must have been difficult for a woman over 40 to have another baby while she battled endlessly with her thoughts. She never recovered from her 58-year-old mother dying of kidney disease. And whatever she went through for two weeks when she was arrested in Prague still clung to her.

For Rosa this was a new life, new country, new husband and now a son. And Dennis was in a good place; he worked all day then headed home to his beautiful wife and son. The first two years were the very best for Dennis and Rosa with me. They continued to work at the café, doing alternate shifts in order to look after me. Rosa was seeing a doctor regularly and had been told to relax and speak with a counsellor when she felt like it. But, for whatever reason—and who knows why or when—slowly the arguing and fighting between Dennis and Rosa escalated.

The front door of the apartment swings open and Rose enters, bouncing off the door jam. She is obviously intoxicated. Dennis stands up from the kitchen table and yells at her, "Where have you been Rosa? Its 9:00 p.m.! You were supposed to be here right after work! Where have you been the last three hours?"

Rosa is trying to listen to him, she is concentrating on him, but feels so confused. She storms into their bedroom and slams the door.

"I'm tired of this! Almost every day now and you never talk to me unless it's some gibberish nonsense! I have no idea what you're talking about!" Dennis yells from the other side of the door. "I am leaving Rosa! Come out of there and let's talk! Please??"

He repeats himself through the door, hoping for a sign. Then the door opens quickly and Rosa, head up high and suitcase in hand, storms out not even acknowledging Dennis till she was almost completely out of the door. She turns around, pops her head inside and looks at me, "Come, Henry! Let's go!"

My dad is crying and looking at me, his arms out to hold me. "Go with your mother, Henry. I will see you real soon. Everything is alright, we just need some space for a bit. Things have been out of hand for too long. We will see each other soon, I promise."

I ran and gave my dad a hug and didn't want to let go, ever. Then a hand came down onto my shoulder and it's my mother.

"Come now, Henry!" she pulls me away and has a firm grasp on my arm.

"Ouch!" I scream as her grasp tightens.

We went to her girlfriend's home to stay till we found a place to live. Two months later, my mom and I moved into some guy's apartment in the west end of Vancouver. My mother would start drinking more with this guy. Petr was a short, chubby guy with a little hair on his head, but a thick of it all over his back and chest. His fingers were stained yellow like his teeth because he smoked three packs of cigarettes a day. Everything smelled and was stained yellow and brown. I never liked him and made it noticeable, which made living with him worse. He wasn't shy about passing on old traditions like beating the crap out of me with his belt or a boot to train me in "proper" manners like he was taught when he was in the army as a kid. My mother would be in tears begging him to stop sometimes, but his rage and drunkenness blinded him from anything else. He would spank me with the belt and beat me with his hands. They would fight and yell at each other constantly, they would drink and just get drunk till they passed out. I hated them both, I hated my life, I missed my dad but hated him for giving up on me.

At age seven I wanted to be dead. I wanted to die.

No one cared about me and I knew it was going to get worse. Mother made no sense anymore. I had gone through three different schools already and it was so difficult to make friends, too. I would stay out with my friends till after dark, sometimes staying hidden at their place from their parents because my friends knew what was in store for me at home. They would smuggle some of their leftovers from their own dinners for me as I kept comfortable in a spare room or storage space in their building. Not knowing any better a few times when I felt I didn't want to continue with my life, I had taken a bottle of Aspirin. Luckily, I would only incur an upset stomach and wake up the next morning.

In school I was constantly having a hard time with authority and teachers. The office was almost a daily visit, which just made life that much more difficult for my mother. Comfort was found through the drugs and alcohol that was introduced to me by the older group of students that I found myself involved with. This masked my inner pains of struggle and the loneliness of feeling unloved by my father. I didn't understand anything that was happening with my mother and all I knew was she abandoned me once before. Why couldn't I just have a normal family? All I wanted was to be happy and loved like I saw at my friends' houses. There was a huge cloud that hovered in my head constantly and it seemed that every time I smiled, that cloud would let it rain, storm in my head.

Chapter 3 – The West End

August 2018 - Downtown Vancouver

STUDIO SEVEN says the sign on the building as I look across the street just at the intersection. I press the WALK button and look down on the piece of paper in my hand. Reading aloud, I say, "Stop now punk! Stop now!" This is the script I'm meant to audition with.

I open the door to the studio and make my way to the desk in the centre of the room. A sexy blonde about 26 years old is filing her nails, chewing gum and talking on the phone. I think, *Shit if she can do all that—chew gum, file nails and talk on the phone—why isn't she a star?* Seriously, she is beautiful and talented in the right places. She hangs up the phone, just as it rings again. She answers and motions me closer and to speak.

"Hello! My name is Henry Bartak and my call time is 3:15," I tell her.

Busy on the phone, she tells the other, "OK! See you then," and hangs up. "Hi Henry, good to see you again! Just have a seat. We are running a bit behind but I know they are excited to see you!" she says with a great big smile.

Her long, blonde, curly hair goes down her back and shoulders. She has big, round blue eyes and it occurs to me just how much I enjoy going to auditions.

"Okay, thanks, no problem. I have time," I replied and took my seat at the corner of the room.

This reminds me of when I was 21 and sitting in the bar I worked at. I always pick the seat against a wall or away from others. Maybe it's a habit from back in my doorman days—I just have to have my back to the wall. Or maybe it's because I love to people watch. Probably both. It's amazing the number of people with the same characteristics at these auditions, and how many beautiful looking people are in this city.

I look at the script and read the highlighted words. *I feel the character. I have this! Just need to be in the moment and relax*, I think. *Reaction and listen*, I keep reminding myself. It is my third callback and this one can make me! This is for a prime time network sitcom and I had a walk on—a few lines here and there—*I can do this easy*. This is the big leagues now and it's what I have been working towards for the last 15 years. I have had several decent opportunities in the past but I was never really ready.

I'm ready now.

I feel it this time. I'm confident from all the live stage acting I have done. Rehearsals upon rehearsals and working on different characters. In 2017 I did seven characters in three theatre productions back-to-back. I love the whole process of theatre productions, all the way from the rehearsal schedule to 14 shows back-to-back. All the auditions, commercials and modeling gigs help—everything helps.

I do miss a lot of the indie film work I did on the island with my good friend, Nathan, and Reimereason Productions. My journey in acting steered me away from a lot of my early bad habits. I want the life I dreamt about when I was younger. I have experienced more now in my life than I thought I would. Each character I took on was a part of me and I reflect to a time in my life in which I had experienced. I mix my early times with the present and, with the lines in a script, draw out a character. I think to myself, *I can do this.* In the beginning I was following a pipe dream of fame cause I know a guy needs a break. But, as I grew into an actor I realized that fame was the real misconception. And my passion for the stage and camera is deeper.

I start to relax and concentrate on being in the moment. Practice my controlled breathing and empty my mind of useless distraction. I need to be spot-on chilled for this audition and sometimes I go to memories of happy things I do in order to be in a Zen mood. *You know the lines now don't think of the lines, be in the moment and trust yourself to react accordingly.*

A couple of times a week I like to go to the local swimming pool, sit in the sauna and swim a few laps. Standing on the edge, I dive as far out as I can with as perfect form as I can. I recall my swim and dive lessons at the West End Aquatic Centre where I was taught when I was younger. Take two inhales and exhales and the last inhale make it the deepest. I would dive down to the bottom of the pool and swim along the floor so when I reached my limit I just pushed up off the floor with my legs and quickly reached the top, breaching the water high into the air like a whale breaching the surface for air. I got such an adrenaline rush taking myself a little farther under water each time. I held my breath and concentrated on my precise movements, trying to achieve as far as I can with less effort so I can go farther and longer. I'd reach out with my arms and hands stretched straight forward as far as I can.

I compare my auditions and holding my breath as I swim the length of the pool under water. I practice discipline, control my thoughts and emotions, and stay focused with precision. I leave the room feeling exhilarated and confident in my decisions, just like reaching the other side of the pool.

To have one's own feelings and distinguish the depths of what makes you feel alive is a fulfillment to me. I am learning as I grow older to be proactive in my life lessons. This is where I am today. Everything I went through growing up and all my mistakes, triumphs, and much soul searching brought me to this point. The exhilarated feeling breaching the water in the pool matches the wonderful feelings before, during and after an audition or having a scene on stage. I long for as much experience as I can get. Memories from my past help me a great deal as well; I figure out who I am and why I am this way. I look deeply at various chapters of my life and each one reminds me of the experience that I went through and how I overcame challenges like growing up in the West End of Vancouver in the seventies and eighties.

"Henry? You may go inside now," the gorgeous blonde behind the desk says with a big smile.

"THANK YOU," I reply, walking by her into the room.

I see a table full of sandwiches and granola bars and fruit everywhere on plates. I look up to see cameras and lights and shades about the room all aimed at a dot on the floor.

"Hello, Henry! We are so happy you have made it today. I am Steven and I am assistant to Drake, our director," a tall, unshaven heavyset guy who has brown curly hair and is wearing a Hawaiian shirt says. He points to the couch at a sharp dressed older gentleman with glasses and a toupee. The man stands up, approaches me and shakes my hand.

"Hi Henry, are you hungry? Want something to drink, perhaps? My name is Drake Phillips," he says.

As I look around the room I see two attractive women who could be make-up and wardrobe. Another older fella in a tan suit with a briefcase is sitting on a stool and I figure he is the money guy. The door opens suddenly and in walks a very tall, stylish, good looking middle aged man wearing pointy black shoes holding a script. Right behind him is a well-built young woman with red—so red!—coloured hair, wearing a matching red skirt holding my headshot and resume. Her heels tap tap tap on the floor as she strides in. They look at me and acknowledge that time is ticking.

"I do apologize everyone! Hi, I am Patty, the producer." She sits beside Drake and Steven on the couch. It's one of those couches that eat people, not firm at all. They all sink into the cushions and I giggle within myself.

"Move over Steven, please?" Patty nudges him with her elbow. "I have no place else to go. Now Henry, can you go on the dot and say hello to Anthony? He will be our camera today. And that's Brim, he will be our reader. Anthony, whenever you are ready."

Steven has had enough fudging about with Patty and decides to stand up. "Ready? Camera rolling, action Henry!" he says.

A few moments later, Steven puts his hand out and I grab it to shake. "Really nice work today, Henry. It shows you know the character. We have two more actors to look at today and we will make a decision by end of the week." He slaps my shoulder to turn me around at the door. "Good work today. I want you in but it is Drake who makes the final decision. You have my vote though."

I nod to him and thank him graciously.

"We will call you by end of this week!" Steven yells at me as I get into the car. I sit down and close my eyes, I breathe, and open my eyes. I have another audition the next morning.

The next day.

Sitting at the back of the room looking down at the script in my hands, waiting for my name to be called, I reminisce about my childhood. Thinking of my father, from vague memories, I recall my fifth birthday and a bicycle in a box he sent me that I had to put together. All I wanted was my mom and dad back together again. This is so ironic because my relationship with Hayden's mom was done by the time he was one year old. And I wanted all of us to be together forever. It broke me spiritually that I had become like my own father. Absent without cause. I call this the Bartak curse. I would fight to be part of my son's life until he was twenty, at which time he decided that I did not do enough for his love and removed me from his life. Hayden wanted no more part of me or the family name and I would not hear from him again.

I have no memories at all of my father when I was younger, but I do have a few photographs of this time. This is nice to see, although I don't recall the times of the photographs.

Years of anger, resentment, hatred and just negativity at every level kept my son and I apart. Looking at the script and going through the scene, I keep thinking of my childhood.

How did I get this way? I flash back to when I was about 7 or 8 years old.

Petr was very much different than the previous men in Mom's life and he drank and smoked much more, too. Life for him was much different when he was my age and back in Czechoslovakia. We left

Ontario when I was about 6. He took my mom and I to Florida in search of a better life, better career for himself, but within only a few weeks of being there, they didn't have much luck finding employment. Money was becoming short, so they decided to try British Columbia, Canada.

In 1977, we moved to Great Northern Way where Petr and Mom started a job as caretakers for The 39 Steps Apartments in East Vancouver. Any recollections I have regarding my past start around this time, but previous memories are blank. I'm not sure why my mother married Petr, cause they always fought. They drank and argued constantly. He never bonded with me and I was just the kid who would go to the corner store to get his cigarettes. Many times his belt came off to "help" me understand what he was telling me. He was indeed a man with old values and beliefs. I always thought he was just mad at me all the time and I was just a bad kid. I always seemed to get into trouble and severely punished for my mistakes. Bruises, bumps and welts were my signs of manhood.

Perhaps my mother felt a lot of guilt about her decisions. Seemed she just did not make any sense some days. She would grab my shoulder, look me in the eyes and tell me stuff. I had absolutely no idea what she was talking about.

"I am supposed to go to the corner of Broadway and fourth at three p.m. and meet Tony," she would say to me. "Tony was working for the government Secret Service and I am to give him this letter." My mother hands me a letter that is sealed, and "Tony" is written on the front.

I knew she was not well, but what is she talking about? Who is this Tony? I know no one will be there because I've given her the benefit of the doubt before and done as she asked, but no one showed up.

At 7 years old I was a very hurt, confused young boy. Just mad and couldn't understand why most things were the way they were. Saturday morning cartoons were what I longed for. I'd watch after school TV and immerse myself in another world. I'd pretend what I saw on TV could actually be in my life. I would think and daydream of another life. *Magnum PI* and *Simon and Simon* were my favs. I dreamt of being a private investigator and I would find my father and ask him why he left. I cherished TV and movies when I was younger.

I recall one time "Henry! Come here!" Petr would bellow from the dining table. "Go to the store and get me two packs of cigarettes and be quick," he would say, handing me the few dollars. Then he poured himself a drink and lit a smoke as he read the newspaper at the dining table. Suddenly he SLAMS the table. "Now!" I turn off the TV and make my way out the door; I know better than to test his patience.

It's a few minutes to walk to the Chinese corner store. I get back home to give Petr his change and smokes. He is in my bedroom and cursing about the state of cleanliness

"Henry! COME HERE!"

I know the tone. I put his cigarettes in my pocket and involuntarily clench my hands.

"Yes, what is it?" I ask as I walk through the doorway.

"What is this? I told you this morning to clean your room. What is this?" he yells.

"I cleaned my room! I don't know why my drawers are on the floor," I reply, scared to death.

I know when I hear his anger I am getting a whipping. And with those thoughts I see his hands go for his belt. I start crying harder, louder, while pleading my case. I beg him to listen, and scream, "Please no!"

"Off with your pants, you know what to do, now do it!!" he would yell at me. "I told you to clean your room and that's what you do! Clean your room!"

The burning stinging slap whip of his belt would strike my bare ass.

"NO!!! Please stop!" I ask in shear pain. SLAP, SLAP, SLAP the belt pounds my rump. I get bright red, swollen welts all over my ass.

"Now clean your room proper," he says as walks out of my room.

Gasping for oxygen and some relief from the pain, I pull my pants up. I dare not sit for a bit, but my legs are weak. I start picking up the drawers on the floor.

"I hate you, I hate you, I wish you were dead. I wish I was dead," I say. *Where is my real father?* I ask myself as I try to breathe.

The door opens and Petr is standing there. "Where are my cigarettes?" he asks me.

I gingerly walk over to my pants on the floor. I reach into the front pocket and pull out his pack of cigarettes, now a little crushed by the attack. I hand them over to him. He looks at the pack, swears and walks out, shutting the door.

A couple of hours later my mother came home from working at a cleaning company. Almost immediately both of them started arguing. While puts dinner together, there's the smell in the air of something burning. More yelling and yelling; I covered my ears.

It was no wonder I sucked my thumb with my right hand and with my left I would hold on to my ear till I was about 9 years old. I guess by doing so I felt some security or comfort? I was a porky, pimply-faced, insecure, scared kid. I was turning 8 and I hated my life. I felt very ugly and insecure. I kept wondering, *Why me? Why doesn't Dad come rescue me?*

Today had to be the worst yet. My mother was home when I came from school.

"Henry, how was school? Are you hungry?" she asked.

"It was OK. Yes I am hungry," I replied.

"Sit down and I have to tell you something," she said, putting her hand on my shoulder and directing me to sit at the table.

"What is it Mom? Is everything okay?" I ask.

"No, it's not alright, Henry. I am sick and must go to the hospital for a while. I have a social worker coming by to take care of you while I am gone..."

My heart stops beating. I am not sure what she just said. Is this true?

"Why?" I ask her.

"I don't trust Petr would take care of you so I called Social Services. I am not well and they want to put me in the hospital for a while. I don't like how Petr hits you so much and we have no where else to go. I am sorry, Henry, but know I love you," she tells me while holding me in her arms. I fall on my knees and break out crying. I beg for her to reconsider. However, I don't want to be left with Petr.

She wraps her arms around me tightly, I feel her tears on my cheek. The social worker is at the door. I quickly run to my room, jump under my covers in my bed and pretend to sleep. A few minutes later I hear two women in the other room. Their voices get louder, footsteps seem to get closer, my eyes are clinched tightly closed when my door opens. I hold my breath, dare not move. Mom pulls the blanket away from my face and looks at me with sadness in her eyes.

I would never see Petr again, though I maintain a close relationship with his daughter, Ivana, to this day. I was taken to a support house and there were many people there. I was beyond scared. I was intimidated by life itself, the different surroundings. I knew no one. I didn't trust anyone and I didn't have my mother anymore. Where is she? I had no way of knowing how to reach her, no knowledge of how long, or why this was all happening. I didn't know how to get a hold of my brothers or my father; I had no one to call for help. I felt on my own.

I cried non-stop for the first several days and then turned my misery to anger. It was mostly directed at anyone around me but also my father. Where was he? Why doesn't he want me? And where is my mother? Why did she let me go? These thoughts and more constantly haunted my mind throughout the days and weeks as I was shuffled through the system.

Weeks turned to months and I kept getting into trouble. I needed to go. I could do it myself. Such a big care facility with so many people. *They'll never know*, I thought. One morning I just walked out the front door. I knew nothing of where I was or where I needed to go. I walked and continued to walk in the rain along the sidewalk as it started to get dark. I came to a strip mall and saw most businesses were closed. But, the laundromat was open. And it's warm and dry. There was one person inside folding clothes. So, I went inside and grabbed a seat by the door. It was quiet and warm. The sounds of the machines working was hypnotic.

Before I knew it I was sound asleep. A few hours later I was awoken by a policeman and taken back to Social Services.

This went on for the next eight months as I entered a few different foster homes and continually ran away from them. I was on the streets around Granville and the Downtown East Side, gradually learning to survive a little more. I didn't want to be in a foster home. People didn't care about me and when I saw an opportunity to escape, I took it.

One day about nine months later I was introduced to a new family. They had a nice home and really spoke genuinely. It was December 1979, close to Christmas. *Maybe this can be... nice.* And for the first time it was. Everyone seemed to care and actually have the time for me. A couple months went by and I felt better mentally.

"Happy birthday Henry!" the whole family yells as I walked into the kitchen.

Wow, I can't believe my eyes.

"Happy birthday to you!" Diane calls out, lunging towards me and giving me a hug. "I made pancakes and bacon, hope you're hungry!" she says to me.

I nod with a big smile on my face.

"I will bake a cake for you today. I hope you have a wonderful birthday!" she says as she walks back into the living room.

I like this place, they are nice people. The other kids are nice, too. I am finally playing with friends. I think I'd like to stay here. The adults said I was changing and they thought I could go back to school soon. Finally, after so long being alone, I felt part of a family.

But, after living there for seven months and it really feeling like a new home to me, one Tuesday morning a social worker came by. When one stops by, everyone in the home stops what they are doing. Everyone holds their breath and acts like puppies in a cage at the pet store; everyone is hopeful it's them getting picked next. Not me; I wanted to stay forever. I see Diane and the other woman speaking and looking at me. Something is up; they call me over.

"Your Mother is coming to take you home right now," Diane said.

"Everything will work out, Henry. Your mother is out of the hospital now and is here to take you back. She has a place for the two of you in the west end. We will miss you, take care of yourself," she said. She hugged me and it would be the last time I saw her. I was so excited to see my mother after so long.

My mother stood by a taxi at the end of the driveway, her arms out wide to hug me. I ran to her as fast as I could and hugged her with all my might. Tears flowed down my face. I am very excited to see my new home, new school and new friends. Is it all true? It was a low income complex in the west end that we moved into (like the welfare families) but I didn't care cause I was home with my mother again.

She was released before but I guess Social Services wanted her to get on her feet before they released me. Soon she got herself a job at the English Bay Café. She had my room made up with a bed and a desk with a chair. The window looked out to the courtyard.

I started in my new school, which was right across the street. Lord Roberts Elementary School would be the first long term school I stayed in. I quickly made friends with classmates who also lived in the complex. My mother seemed so happy and her new job was good. I would soon be growing up like a normal kid.

On my 11th birthday my mother surprised me with a trip to Australia! She had a brother and a couple nieces there that she had not seen in almost 25 years. Australia was so very far away, what an adventure. For the most part I didn't care for it all, it was all so different. I still had so much hurt inside me that I had difficulty understanding most of all this. But the time I had with this foreign family of my mother's—especially the time with my Uncle and cousins—was the best. I got real close with my Uncle Narcis and my two female cousins, Michelle and Magda. We went for three months and we almost stayed; I wish we had, looking back. But, we came home because of me. I missed my new friends. I made a real bad fuss for my mom, which I later regretted., This trip though made things really great after, for a while anyways.

My mother was doing better and soon had girlfriends stopping by for visits. And soon a boyfriend, Frank. I didn't like him at all. He was a tall, rough looking thick man with great big hands. He was a butcher and he drank and smoked like Petr. But, still no signs of my father. Why? Does he not know where I am? I was looking for answers or distraction—not sure which—but I was still so confused when I thought of my life.

A good escape from reality for me was to go downtown to Granville street with my friends. I enjoyed going to movies and sneaking through to see more than one at the Capitol Six Theatre. I would sit and watch two or three movies in a day for free. I entered a new life through the stories on the screen. My first experience with a famous person happened in the Denman Inn Hotel, which was just down the block from where we lived. I met Ron Howard and his new family twice, Mr. Roper from *Three's Company*, and the villain side kick Ned Beatty from *Superman*. I was always so taken by their presence.

Watching television was always important to me, cause watching the shows let me dream. I dreamt of a better place with fun and adventure. I incorporated my weekly favourite character into my daily life using an accent or gesture, a look or movement. One morning, my best friend and I were involved as extras in a movie called *Natty Gann*, which was being filmed just couple blocks away. It was just one day and probably only a couple hours worth, but this made me feel so wonderful. Like anything was possible. *This is where I should be*, I thought. But, I would not have another opportunity till many years later.

Our lives changed slowly up to 1983. Frank moved in with us. I admit I had a burning hole in my heart for my past and I saw a repeat of history and I was not going to just surrender to circumstance but fight for my mom and me. I never truly appreciated the small things I had. Like having my mother in my life again. I always inquired about my father, but without any contact I found anger and resentment instead. I was constantly bullied by older kids in the neighbourhood who would tease me because of my pimples and fat tummy. But, at the time it was just the way it was. In turn, I bullied others that I felt I could intimidate. A circle of punishment and anger came to me and I give it back. Soon, I hung with a group of senior students in the school and participated in their activities. Whether it was stealing, vandalism or smoking pot, drinking, fighting and breaking the laws. Break-ins and shoplifting were normal. Fighting for turf and supporting our own was daily life in the west end. We had a small group with skateboards and we would cruise the underground parking lots for opportunities.

"Hey! Stop! Hey you!" yells some guy coming out the exit door into the parkade.

He sees me crouched down half in the car with broken glass all over the concrete floor. He starts walking faster towards me so I grab my skateboard and jump over the railing to the next parking level. Couple other guys in our group are doing the same.

"RUN!!" I yell.

We always had a route out, and we ran for it. A fire escape just on the second level, we jump one and climb to the next floor up. There you run like hell out the front gate and up into the streets.

Unbeknownst to me, my mother was gradually becoming mentally ill again. Not knowing what to do or the signs to look out for, and with no help from me, she would eventually need care and be admitted to the emergency at St. Paul's Hospital. My older step brothers took turns taking care of me. We visited Mom one time and when I first saw her in the ward for mental illness patients my heart broke for her. Frank moved out very soon after—like a few weeks later. Thankfully.

Tomas picked me up from school one day and took me to see our mother. He told me she was in Riverview again. She was in a straight jacket and was being helped to the visitor's lounge by the nurse.

"I am sorry but for her safety we need to keep this on her until she is in her room. I will just be over here if you need me," the nurse said while helping Mom into the chair. She took a seat at the table next to us. Mom looked tired and doped up. Her hair was a bit messy and she had patient's pants with slippers on. I started crying obsessively and wanted to leave. She smiled at me and told me everything would be alright.

"I'm feeling better, Henry. Be good and I will be home soon, OK?" she said, brushing her hand over my head. "You are always my favourite son, I am sorry for the way I am."

A couple weeks went by and Mom came home again. She seemed fine and well to me. I was really confused, angry and sad by then and I continued to get in trouble by hanging with the older crowd in the neighbourhood. The police constantly picked me up and brought me home. I was shoplifting in all the major department stores in downtown Vancouver: Sears, Eaton's and Hudson's Bay. I got caught once in the Eaton's store and they had me locked up downstairs in their holding cells. Mom had to come to get me out. It was really embarrassing for her and I felt like I let her down.

This was when I encountered Asian gangs. Guns and gang fights. Downtown Vancouver was like my backyard and Stanley Park was my front. I constantly ran away from home for days and I hung out with older friends. We looked out for one another. There was Scott, he was one of the oldest, and lived with his brother and father in a house a block away. Jaakko was a Finnish guy who I had been friends with since Grade Four; he was our big guy (along with me). Frankie was a short, wiry kid from across town. Gordon was my best friend, he was tall and blonde; a good looking guy. To me it was like another family. By now the local police were quite familiar with us and I was constantly being brought home. This devastated my mother and didn't make her life easy.

Somewhere at the beginning of our summer holidays in '82 I started my very first job. I was a dishwasher in a restaurant in the west end of Vancouver. I got the job because my friends and I were playing in a small park off Nicola Street—actually we were "acting." Whenever someone came down the sidewalk we would pretend that Jaakko, Gordie and Frankie were beating the crap out of me. Someone always called the cops, at which point we would all take off in different directions. It was a game we played. But, this time a tall woman with long wavy blonde hair came up and said, "Hey! You kids! Stop it! You guys bored or what? Who wants a job? I just opening my restaurant and I could use some help!"

The four of us looked at each other and burst out laughing.

"Hey! I'm serious here, who like a job?" she says again.

We stopped laughing and looked at each other again.

"Hey this is a good opportunity to make some money, legit like."

I put my hand up. She told me to come in the next day for my first shift. I worked there all summer. It was the best individual positive experience I'd ever had. I opened my first bank account and for the first time I didn't need to steal what I wanted. I did anyways.

In March 1983, just after my 13th birthday, I had a normal day at high school. As usual, I was fleeing the older boys who wanted to kick my butt.

"C'mon Henry! Just stop—we want to kick your ass! Ha ha ha!" They yelled and laughed as they quickened their stride. "C'mon Henry, stop!"

My legs were just doing the best they could to carry this plump, pimple-faced kid. One block, two blocks—*Are these guys going to quit?* I'm breathing so hard snot is running down my face. Home is another three more blocks.

"Motherfucker! We going to get you!" I hear behind me.

I just about can't take any more, and just like that they are gone. I look behind me all over the streets. I make it to my complex and walk the stairs to my door.

"Hi Mom! Mom? Are you here?" I ask as I enter.

I look in the living room and kitchen. *Guess not.* I put my school bag in my room, hit the fridge and turn the TV on. I figure she's working late again or something. She will be home soon, I know. I finish watching after school funny cartoons and I'm excited for the next show when the phone rings.

"Hello? No, sorry she is not home. Can I take a message?" I reply to the caller and shortly hang up and I wonder just where is she?

Maybe she is in her room? I never did look there. I opened the door to her bedroom and looked inside.

Oh! She is sleeping. I see her lying on her back on top of the blankets.

"Mom, you awake? There was a phone call for you," I said to her. "Mom!" I said a little louder.

I got closer to her side of the bed and saw she was on top of her covers and a bunch of whitish bubble goo is leaking from her wide open mouth.

"MOM!!!" I yell at her as I grab her shoulder and give her a nudge. She wasn't opening her eyes! She was not moving! "MOM WAKE UP!!"

I ran to the phone in the living room and called Jaakko. "Jaakko! My mom is dying, please help me!! My mom is dying!! Call an ambulance please hurry!!" I was crying into the phone telling Jaakko's parents.

His parents called an ambulance and came to get me. They knew my mom and the challenges we faced. The ambulance came and medics tried to save her life. She was trying to kill herself by swallowing pills; seems life is too difficult for some. She lived, but I didn't see her for few days after.

Tomas drove to the hospital. It seemed like in one day my life was changing again. After the emergency ward, my mom was admitted to Riverview again. I would stay with Tomas and his new wife in Maple Ridge. It was far from the city I was used to. I was not sure when I would see my mom again. I never even said goodbye to my friends or my other family from school. Never had the opportunity to explain what happened, where I was going, and that I would miss them all so very much.

There was so much anger and resentment building up inside me and I was still sad and very confused. Too many questions with no answers. I missed my mom. I hated my dad and worst of all I just wanted to be home again. Just Mom and me, please?

I would never live with my mother again. It was a dozen more years till I went back to the west end of Vancouver. She finally got better after several months of care. But, by then I was too much for anyone to handle. And I think it was best that Mom tried to remain in positive SPIRITS. I am not sure how long she spent at Riverview—months? Maybe over a year. But, she would eventually be released and have to start a new life for herself once again. This time without me, and on her own.

"Henry Bartak! Henry Bartak! You're next."

I snap out of my thoughts and look up. I wave at the young lady who is searching the room for me.

"Thank you, you're next," she says. I take a few deep breaths and look down at the script.

I have this.

Several minutes later I am shaking hands with the middle aged lady who directed me through the audition. "Great improv, Henry, nice and natural. You will hear from us in a couple of days," she says to me. I smile and feel exhilarated. I nailed it. As I walk out, I think, *Why not me?* I I have this!

Chapter 4 – I am a Pisces

A quote from the internet explains something little about who I am. "Pisces are selfless. They are always willing to help others without hoping to get anything back. Pisces is a water sign and as such this zodiac sign is characterized by empathy and expressed emotional capacity. Their ruling planet is Neptune, so Pisces are more intuitive than others and have an artistic talent."

I so am a Pisces. Funny thing is, it describes me exactly. I have been swimming 2 to 3 times per week at the local recreational centres for the last 20 years. I just love the exercise, relaxation and meeting people with the same interests. The freedom of swimming underwater opens my imagination. I went snorkeling in Jamaica and it was an unbelievable feeling. It's like you're alone on another planet.

The artistic talent must be why I became an actor. Or maybe it was how I found talent in surviving my childhood, always pretending to be someone else. I constantly imitated the little "things" that an individual does. Like speech patterns, a habit, an action of theirs that I found interesting. I would study how someone walks down the street or makes a movement that is unique to them and then make it my own. It's probably why I enjoy character acting and physical comedy the most. Seems easy for me to be someone else, cause to be me I need to go somewhere else. I need to go inside my history, which I try to bury deep inside. I have blocked most of my past and try to not let it interfere with my present. I truly believe acting saved me. I am empty without it and challenged by it, which makes me feel alive and with purpose.

I caught the acting bug in June 2003. I was operating a rubber tire backhoe for a construction company in Nanaimo, BC. I worked in civil excavation and was talking to a home owner about landscaping his yard when we started chatting about life in Nanaimo. He was an older man, short, with glasses and very friendly. We spent several minutes enjoying our conversation.

"Henry, you ever think about the acting industry?" he asked me.

I laughed! "Me? An actor? No, I can't say that was ever on my radar," I replied.

"You should. You have a good, friendly personality about you, plus a great look about you. You can play many different roles," he said quite seriously.

"I don't even know where to start," I said.

He reached into his pocket, pulled out a business card and handed it to me. *Spotlight Talent Agency Film and TV Acting School* it said.

"Give the lady a call. She is very talented, kind and helpful," he said.

I thought it was a joke. But, if there's one thing I have learned, it's always Go For It! One door closes, another opens. You just never truly know what's out there; if an opportunity exists you should take the chance. Also, listen to what others are telling you. They are on the outside looking at you and they have a different view.

A month went by, I thought *What if?* everyday. Pisces are dreamers, and I honestly am. I have seen people's stories and how their dreams came true. So, I know it can happen.

Why not me? Like seriously? Why not me?

If I put out the maximum effort, can't I have a happier life? I know I can do this, it is challenging for sure. I love watching or reading stories of the underdogs who triumph. I see myself just like these people who have gone through hardship and failures but continue to move forward because it was who they were on the inside.

I called the number on the card and spoke with a hurried, to-the-point woman with an English accent; she had an atmosphere of greatness about her. I told her why I called and she invited me to her school.

"I have zero experience with acting," I said.

"It's why I have an 'on camera' acting class for beginners," she said.

Jacqui was a beautiful curly blonde haired woman with an English accent who was a serious, fast paced, down-to-business acting coach. She was so passionate about what she did. And best of all she was very interested in sharing her knowledge with anyone who came to her. In this small home out in the sticks on Vancouver Island was this highly dynamic, experienced, kind woman. She was married to an ex-NHL player and ran a school. She spread the love of acting to numerous people and provided hope and education. I took night classes for almost 18 months, mainly cause I was no natural. I sucked bad!

I had no idea of what it took to become an actor. But, with Jacqui's experience and tons of patience, I finally felt secure enough to start on film. She introduced me to real filmmaking in progress as an extra. I fell in love with all the positive vibes on a set with people who all felt the same way I did. I worked five years as an extra, acting with people I saw on television or film. Kirsty Alley, Lou Diamond Phillips, Dean Cain, Sissy Spacek, Kim Bassinger and more—over 20 projects and numerous skilled people. I loved this new adventure and was so glad I took the chance to call Jacqui that very first time.

On set one day in 2005 I had lunch with Lou Diamond Phillips; speaking with him was so exciting. We were to do a scene together after lunch and we discussed the scenario. He was so friendly and open and I, for the first time in my life, felt important. We were navy sailors, he the detective and I the extra, but after our lunch together I had so much hope for a better, happier life to come. I felt that this was my destiny, that I was finally doing something right.

"You have a great look about yourself. Stick with it and do many versatile roles and you will make it," he told me as we munched on sandwiches.

I was in awe. And will never forget his pleasant nature and advice.

Every day I learned more about who I was and what I could draw upon from inside of me in order to become someone else. There was so much negative stuff in my other life that acting and being on set was therapeutic to me. I had so much hope for my future and I was willing to give it all I had. I have taught myself a hell of a lot of who I am through this and continue to have hope because of it. I tried to gain as much experience as possible; I wanted to be a winner, a successful winner. I thought if I tried stage acting, that my auditions and film acting would become easier and I would become a decent working actor. So, I took any role that was offered, no matter if it was paid or volunteer. And I was getting better, and I was learning how to be me.

Wasn't too long before I stepped up to speaking roles and found the excitement of my name on the door to my very own room in the trailer. No, not the trailer but a room. This was an accomplishment and I was proud of myself. My roles were getting bigger and more challenging and I loved every moment.

I have been taught to always give back to others as I have been given to by some. Thirteen theatre productions, numerous film and television appearances, modeling gigs, and now writing—I have a new addiction that I can actually live with for rest of my life. Watch for the signs, follow your heart and be honest with yourself are but a few pieces of advice I agree with. No regrets but sometimes you need to burn bridges, end friendships, move somewhere else, take the chance at your dreams. Sometimes things don't work out, but it just shows you how badly you want your dream to come true. Patience is a must, don't give up. Ever, cause then you regret. And always be considerate to others, be kind and respectful cause you just never know who, for example, the receptionist may be. She could be the director's wife who is helping out when the normal receptionist is sick. "Life is too short" is not just a motto; you must live it.

Is there a higher power? Perhaps. I believe people cross our paths for a reason, and that what doesn't break you makes you stronger. There is more out there than we give credit for: god, guardian angels, karma, UFO, ghosts. All my beliefs come from my own experiences. I've had more than my fair share and I'm still seeking more.

I saw an unidentified flying object in 2016. At first, I thought it was a planet. On a hot August afternoon, I went out to my balcony and saw this round object way high in the sky. It was much too early yet for stars. About twenty minutes later, it started to move in a straight line, quickly heading north over the mountains and out of sight. Just so quickly it was gone.

One time, my close friend's parents in Victoria passed away and I was helping him move their possessions out of an old heritage home near Beacon Hill Park. I decided to stay behind and get the next load ready as Chris and a couple other friends left to unpack the first truck full. All was quiet and I was admiring the old characteristics of the home when I distinctively heard heavy footsteps upstairs walking down the hallway. My ears perked up and goosebumps jumped onto my arms. I slowly walked up the stairs and listened carefully for more sounds. There was no one there. *I am the stupid fucker investigating sounds alone, like in a horror movie*, I thought.

Another time, I encountered weird sounding SPIRITS at the Little Theatre in Ladysmith, BC. It was about 4:00 p.m. on a weekday in fall. Wendy, a nurse from Nanaimo who also directed and acted, and I were in this old one room school house built in 1912. It was a school that was turned into a dinner theater by a retired couple who acted all their lives. They cooked, directed, acted, wrote, produced, and even operated this theatre group. Wendy and I were in early for extra rehearsal on our scenes. Now Wendy, may I say, is extremely intellectual and a superb actress. I felt honoured to be acting alongside her. We had all heard stories from fellow members who experienced something weird in the past, like a warm breath on your neck when no one is around or a hand on your shoulder while doing makeup. Things moving, sounds and sightings were common there. In mid-line, we both heard a little girl laughing— clearly and loudly. We immediately stopped and listened.

"Hello?!" I said. No answer. "You heard that, right?" I asked.

"Yes, I think someone is here," she replied.

I walked into every room and even outside all the around the school and no one was there.

"I heard this place was haunted, now we know for sure," I said.

"Yes, this is scary," she replied.

I decide to look around the building and find the source of the laughter. After walking through every room and checking outside around the building I never found anything. We started rehearsing again and never heard anything after. The cast showed up one by one and we shared our experience with them. It wouldn't be the last time I encounter strange situations.

News from Australia, Narcis passed away in a construction accident, My mother and I were devastated. I met him when I was 11 years old when my Mother took me to meet him we kept in touch. He was really nice to me, understood me and we bonded. I know that he became my guardian angel and has been watching over me since. Several times I've gone left, for example, and people who went right died. I don't know why, for what purpose am I here, or what I'm supposed to become or do.

I do know that I should have been dead many times (like my story about Brad and the ill-fated boat ride—later) but escaped without a scratch and I credit my Uncle Narcis, my guardian angel, for having my back. Most recently at work while operating an excavator I accidentally broke through a 240 volt hydro line that powered the on site crane. I am totally fortunate that nothing happened to me. An angel? Fate? Karma? Good luck? Who knows for sure but I like to think that my uncle is looking out for me.

Fortunately for me, I was taught life lessons really fast and hard, but I definitely lacked lifelong lessons never taught to me from a childs parents. I would say just the last ten years or so I have learned how to live a normal life. When I was 36 and figuring out what to do with myself, I thought *Why didn't I ever think of buying a house?* But by then I had started my second bankruptcy and knew my thoughts were a tad bit late in life. Wish I had been shown a different way of life earlier but a person should not dwell on the past. Instead use the experiences to build yourself a better tomorrow.

A person never stops learning and is taught many lessons, but some are definitely stronger than others. As each year goes by the lessons seem to have more impact on my life. So I turn to other people and their stories of life, trials and tribulations and look at how they overcame adversity. I draw strength from watching others succeed. There was no one except my mother the first ten years that showed me any other way. I looked at my idols on television and in the movies and began to appreciate music more in my 30s. I appreciate it for the words, stories and the people behind those wonderful songs. I've listened to on the radio my whole life. Recently I have been really taken by Gord Downie from The Tragically Hip, and his story. What a true Canadian inspiration.

I make my bed every single morning before I leave for work. I clean my own dishes, floors, windows, toilet and home on a regular basis. I wouldn't say I am a neat freak or have some character disorder that requires everything must be put in a certain place, but I appreciate a nice, welcoming home to live in. I collect western native art mostly because of my close collection of friends who are western native carvers. A western coastal theme with native plants, art, and furniture surrounds my existence in my life. Tomas gave me a coffee table made by his Italian father-in-law. It is made of a six-foot-long cut slab of red cedar coated with many layers of resin for a beautiful, clear, solid protective covering over the entire surface. The legs of the table are one solid piece of the tree roots and are also covered in clear resin. I love being Canadian and the freedom that my parents felt here in order to continue living in this great place.

I have started over many times and I always hated letting go of my possessions in order to continue moving forward. Three steps back and one step forward seems to be normal for me. I learned something new about myself every time I had to go through something.

Live it like it's your last day. If you can't do anything about it then don't sweat it. But, try at least so you know in your heart that it does matter. I did the best I could do at the times when I was challenged the most. Love is a very strong emotion and the consequences are the best and worst feelings I have encountered. I have longed for the love of a woman since the first day of my mother's absence. Over the years, it seems easier to be alone even though I am fighting with myself and the longing of a woman's presence. It's just everything about them that I miss.

Chapter 5 – The Terminator, 1984

I left my life in the west end of Vancouver halfway through my first year in high school (Grade 8) and I started again in the country. Maple Ridge is an hour outside of Vancouver and I started at a new school near there Garibaldi Secondary School. Missing my old friends from Vancouver immensely, I endured mass depression and thoughts of *Why me?* constantly flooding my brain. Looking back now, I had become so damaged, so quickly, so young.

The summer before, I was constantly hanging out with my friends and being introduced to skateboarding and the preppie and punk styles of the time. With my summer job, I had money to actually buy—not steal—new and trending clothes. And as I was learning about myself and fitting in with a close group of friends, I found myself on the complete opposite of my position in society. Now, as a preppy/punk skateboarding kid, I was surrounded by country farm folks. I stood out like a clown at a KKK meeting. I was a big kid who never smiled and wasn't afraid of anyone; why should I be afraid? Deep inside I was torn in half, one side begging for a rescue and someone to love me and the other side begging to be let go of the struggles and just die already.

Almost immediately I was defending myself and fighting for my right to be me. Luckily, I was not the only outsider at the school. There was a very small group that also appreciated the "punk rockers" of the school. There was Keith, a short, blonde, nice-looking kid who lived with his mother down the street. Dean, a taller kid with a mohawk and acne was the centre of our group. He never spoke much of his upbringing, just said it was rough and not nice. Bradley was a chubby, short guy with red hair as long as a chick's—it was down his back. And then Amanda: blonde with streaks of purple one week, blue another. Always changing her hair colour and styles. We all wore ripped, bleached jeans, army boots from the surplus stores, and patches of rock bands covered our ripped up jean jackets. Skateboards were our transportation of choice. We hung out in the smoking pits at school in our own way. Always inviting recruits new to school.

By the end of that school year, I was involved in dozens of fights with guys trying to prove themselves to their peers. Usually farm guys that grew up here. Hence, I acquired the nick name "The Terminator." The movie had just been released and I suppose I had a resemblance to Arnold Schwarzenegger at the time. I was also introduced to new drugs and much more alcohol. We would pick mushrooms in the cow fields, or go to downtown Vancouver for acid, cocaine, opium, hash. Trying to adjust and continue to smother any emotion was my only goal. I seriously had no use for school and actually being taught something useful. I was just surviving.

Tomas had just married his girlfriend, Daniela, and they bought a home on Smith Avenue, just a few minutes from the high school. Daniela had just graduated from Garibaldi Secondary a couple years prior and Tomas was working towards a career already. They bought the home on Smith Avenue that year with the intentions of starting their family when I fell into their laps. I brought all my emotional baggage from the city with me. As well as my big city attitude of not giving a fuck. I really appreciated my brother's help and I longed for a relationship of love and understanding just like he had.

But, I was very mixed up in my head and most of the time I felt I never deserved any love from no one. Yet, I searched for it with several girls in my new school. My interest in girls came way back in elementary school. Growing up in the west end in the 70s meant very free-minded people with parents who lived through the 60s.

My first sexual encounter was in Grade 6 when I took a friend (we'll call her "M") to a movie. She had long, blonde wavy hair all 70s style, a cute button nose and round green eyes with chubby little cheeks. Just down right cute and feminine as a teen girl can be. Every boy in school was in love with her. We met outside her apartment and walked to the Odeon on Granville. We wanted to see *Return of the Living Dead Part 2*. On the way, we sparked a joint she had sneaked from her mother. We sat up in the balcony for the weekday matinee. The theatre was quite empty. I was so nervous and so anxious to kiss her. Her tits were the biggest in school that year and just as the movie started I knew I had to try. I pulled out the old yawn-and-stretch-the-arms routine and my arm fell on her shoulders. She quickly adjusted herself in her seat and placed her head on my chest. Her hand had nowhere else to go but on my knee. I was so god damn nervous both about being rejected or—worst of all—actually going through with whatever was next.

A few minutes went by and the movie lights up the screen but I'm not paying attention. Her hair smelled so fucking good. Oh my god, I was getting a boner. I'm committed at this point I figure, no backing off now. Pretending I am watching the movie, my hand shifts to her breast. Geezers! My hand is on her boob! And she's not saying anything! Oh, it's so squishy and big, I massage her a little more. *This movie is great!*, I think. All of a sudden, she places her other hand right on my crotch, and it's trying to break out of the zipper. She massages me through my jeans and I'm squirming in my seat. We decide to adjust to more comfortable and easier access for ourselves. By now, my hand is in her shirt and I'm touching a bare boob. I am on Cloud 9. We're locked lips and breathing heavy. It's getting warm, I must say.

She unzips my jeans and grabs me as I try to get my other hand between her legs. I dare not let go of her breast, it feels so good. Whatever she is doing to me it feels wonderful and new. I feel like I'm growing up a bit. My hand makes it to her sweet spot, but I'm not quite sure what I'm supposed to do from here. She is so warm and moist, I feel her hairs. Oh my god this is truly happening. Then just as we both are super hot, the movie ends. Immediately, the lights are on, people down front of us are getting up and leaving. The odd person is looking up our way, probably they knew. I wave at them and we giggle. We decide we can't leave, so we stay for the next movie. More people coming in and sitting down, we never let our temperatures drop. We stayed till about halfway through the second show. I will never forget *Return of the Living Dead Part 2*. The girls I met at school were all so very special in every way to me and would always be part of the beautiful times in my life.

Other extra-curricular activities while adjusting to this new country life of mine got me in trouble. On many occasions. I had lots of issues with authority and teachers; I was more lost than ever. Kind of like swimming underwater doing somersaults and not knowing which way is up. Constantly being sent to the office for being a class clown, distraction to others, swearing, just causing shit in class. My attention was limited and school just seemed like a process I just had to get through. Quickly though, I made friends and was getting more into music. I loved Rock 'n Roll, Heavy

Metal, and the 1980s music scene. My ripped, bleached jeans turned into regular tight blues. I grew my hair and was making quite an impression in my new place. My circle of friends grew in variety. I still enjoyed my punk side but had a closer connection with Dayton who wore blue jeans and a leather jacket—kind of like *The Outsiders* style.

We were long-haired rockers now, wearing Iron Maiden, AC/DC and Led Zeppelin badges on the backs of our Storm Riders. All week my buddies and I went to school and got through the week saving up what money we could for Friday night. We would all pitch in and go for a drive to the "Zellers Drive Thru." That's what we called the Zellers department store in the town of Haney. We'd drive up to the front of the building and there were a good dozen dealers standing out front. We pull up alongside them slowly with the windows rolled down.

"Red hair! Thai! Cambodian!" was called out to us from each person we slowly pass by. Their hands out showing us joints, packages, blots of paper.

"Acid! Shrooms!"

Other cars were in front and behind us at the "Drive Thru at Zellers." We would pause at our favourite dealer and grab a dime bag. Quickly someone would be all set to roll up a doobie as we drove off to the liquor store. Back then, 20 bucks between a few of us would set us up with a bag of weed or chunk of hash, a bottle of booze or case of beers, and a pack of smokes! We would search for parties or just find some place to hang out and get wasted.

I still had a big shield surrounding me and my emotions. Too much had happened in my short life so far and getting wasted whenever I could helped me get through many days where I was so lost. My weeks started on Monday morning going to school, and making it to Friday seemed such a struggle that I would find someone to celebrate with. Friday night would turn to Saturday nights with as much blurr and buzz as I could obtain. This became the routine for the next 15 years.

My friends became so close to me and were the family I needed. Living with my brother and his new wife never truly felt like my home. I knew it was short term and his wife and I never really bonded well. Could you blame her? Looking back, I was a shit. She had her life starting now. She was from a family of old country culture Italians and most of her family lived close by. By the end of Grade 8 I was told I had to leave my brother's place and find somewhere else to go. I was always getting into trouble at the school, constantly fighting. I would beg, borrow and steal whatever I could just to be able to get wasted with my buddies. I was very thankful for my good friend, Kenton, and his older brother for talking their mother and step father into fostering me. At this time, I was one of the youngest people to be recognized by social services and with their help I was able to pay my rent. Even though all I had was a couch in their living room, it was a warm, dry place for me to sleep. But, as soon as the school year ended they decided to move to Pitt Meadows, which was the next town over.

Kenton and I had to start in a new school—a rival school from ours. We quickly made our mark, though, and we had allies within the school; it did not take us long to bond. I was quickly centred-out from the rest cause I had no parents. This was a huge family-oriented town and some parents of my new friends were very protective of their kids. Meaning, they were told not to hang out with me cause I was trouble. I looked like trouble, I had no rules, no discipline, no parents and I admit I had a look about me—an emotionless look—and I didn't smile much. People said I scared the shit out of them just with my look. But, once people got to know me they found out I was harmless.

"The best thing you can do is be his friend. He is a great guy when you get to know him. He watches your back any time," I was once told by a couple of friends. The ones who felt something with me became my family and a few are still close to me now.

A couple of my friends' parents embraced me right away and took me in. Their doors were always open to me, whether it be the front door of their home or the door to their fridge. I gladly accepted a hand out of a meal. A good meal was hard to come by, I was still learning to boil water for mac and cheese. My group of friends grew a little more in this new town. I seemed to have found a new home once again. The new home Kenton's parents had was just not the home for me. I still had the couch to sleep on in their family room. Everyone else had their own rooms in their brand new home at the end of the cul-de-sac. The family room was located by the door to the garage, where at night they would put their little fucking yappy dog who would whine constantly and scratch at the door. This drove me mad and I would try to sleep anywhere else I could without going back there.

One day I was introduced to Kevin, an older guy who had inherited a home from his parents who were killed in an accident. He was in his twenties and working, and was the absolute opposite of me and my friends. He stayed in his room most of the time, never drank alcohol or did drugs. Kind of nerdy type to us at the time. But, he was very compassionate and kind and, through some convincing from Christopher, a big aggressive bear of a guy who was dating Lara (Kenton's older sister; she was tall, slender and sexy for an older woman in her twenties). Christopher got to know me the predicament at Kenton's home. He was like an older brother to me and we bonded well. The house was on the edge of town, by the Pitt River Bridge. Kevin agreed to rent me a room and share his home with me. By 1986 at the age of 16, I was renting my own place. I took the school bus into town every day, even though I would usually get kicked out of school shortly after lunch time or I just skipped. I could never "get" into school, you know? Homework? Can't be bothered. Friends and hanging out with the people who embraced me filled a void.

I was peddling whatever I could make a few bucks on: weed, acid, pills. Getting numb also gave me a distraction from everyday loneliness. Looking back, I had no direction and no one truly looking out for my future. There were always teachers or social workers who gave their advice and tried to steer me in the right direction but it just never stuck with me. I would pull anyone towards me who wanted to be numb, too. I gave a third of the school soccer team free acid on the bus to an away game in Langley. I wasn't even part of the team, just my closest friends were. It was something you might see today in a film, boy oh boy. The goaltender, Duane, my closest friend even to this day, was higher than a kite. He was on the field in uncontrollable laughter and eyes bulging out with pupils dilated. They won that game behind his spectacular saves; his physical limitations seemed to not exist. The bus ride home was something from *Animal House* except the party was on the bus! Scott, one of our closest friends, mooned a group of cars passing by. He was always the kid on the wild side, and he died too young.

One day I was at my locker between classes. There were five minutes to change books and hit the next one. I noticed this cute girl about four lockers over getting her books as well.

"Hi! How goes it? What class you have?" I asked her while rummaging through my locker.

"Excuse me?" she replied.

"What's your name?" I asked her.

"Oh, Deanna," she whispered without even glancing at me.

I couldn't help it, my eyes were locked on. She had a typical 80s do, her hair was long, red and curly in some parts; it cascaded down both sides of her freckled face.

"What class you have next?" I asked her again.

"The same class you have, Henry. I sit behind you a couple seats. English." She said this as she turned to face me with an innocent smile and her perky nose. She closed her locker door. "Don't be late again," she said as she walked away.

She knows my name? I had to ask her to the Valentine's dance in the auditorium that Friday!

I couldn't stop turning around in my seat, and I was pissing off the teacher.

"Henry! One more and you can go to the office!" The teacher slammed the metre stick on his table. I turned around and everyone in class was laughing at me. I didn't care. I longed for the attention from my classmates. I was used to being centred out, the class ass, clown, instigator all my school years.

"Ok! Relax!" I reply to him.

I heard whispers behind me and little giggles.

"Pssst..." I heard behind me. A hand is by my shoulder and holding a piece of paper. I grabbed it just as teacher Standanko turned around. With my hands down in my lap, hidden by my desk, I unfolded the piece of paper. "Quit turning around, don't get kicked out. Are you going to the dance?" is written and it's signed with a happy face and a capital "D." Just then the bell rang and everyone rushed for the door. I time getting up from my chair to just when she walked past me.

"Hi!" I said. "Yeah, I'm going are you?"

"Yes, I'm going," she replied.

"Great! Then we can go together, maybe?" I said. I'm right up tight to her and a few more students as we squeeze through the door.

"OK!" she yelled out as she quickly walked down the hall the opposite direction of where I was going.

I was so excited! I couldn't get her off my mind the rest of the day. Every time I went to my locker I waited to see her at her locker. She was so different than any other person I had met. She had a genuine softness to her persona and a smile that locked my eyes on her lips. I knew as soon as I saw her that I had to win her heart.

I found out soon after that she had a huge secret crush on me since I had first come to the locker next to hers. We started to be together immediately. She had to sneak out or lie to her father and step mother in order to see me. I would be waiting outside on the streets of her strata complex. Her father had heard about me, as most parents with kids going to the high school knew who I was. Deanna was absolutely forbidden to see me and sometimes she got caught. Her father would ground her for a few nights. But, we saw each other every time we could. We were drawn to each other in every way.

My older friend Christopher had a Jeep Wagoneer and he let me use it to take Deanna out on a "date." We usually went to a dark corner at the end of road and made out for hours. I was her first and I wanted us to be together forever. We loved each other like I have never experienced before. Her father found out that she was still seeing me and was truly upset about it. Deanna was getting caught in the middle of having to choose, and either way someone would be upset. Nothing could come between us or our love.

The new friends in Grade 9 were closer even than those in Vancouver. The house I lived in was a two story and a basement. Kevin kept to his own room and didn't mind my friends coming over. We usually sat in my room smoking weed and having some drinks before heading out for the night to party. My friends would bring over leftovers for me all the time cause they knew I didn't have much food. Other times they asked their parents and there were a few kind and understanding parents who were genuinely concerned for my welfare. It was really tough for me and most every night I would pray to God that my life would get better. That my dad would rescue me. But, there was nothing coming and I feared that much.

I would drink excessively and smoke cigarettes and pot till everything I had would be gone and done that night. Wouldn't matter if it was a 26 or 40 or 60oz, it was done. Acid, mushrooms, cocaine, pills, booze, weed, opium; just whatever I got my hands on. The exceptions were heroin and steroids. I never was interested them. But, I would drink a lot. By myself or with others, it never mattered. My intoxication always intensified when Deanna was forbidden to see me. Days went by and I would not hear from her. There were days I wished I was dead already because the constant misery that clouded over me kept getting darker with stronger and louder thunder storms. I survived because of the support of my friends that always called or showed up at just the right times.

Why not me?

By the summer of '86 I felt I had lived a life already. I felt older than I was. On the way to Expo 86 in East Vancouver I decided I was truly old enough.

"Hey Duane! Hold up here, I'm going inside," I told him.

We were heading west towards Main and Hastings when I saw a store front with a sign that read Star Tattoo and I darted inside. A guy with long, dark hair and a big mustache sat at the counter; he was covered all over with tats. Another tattooed guy with blue jeans, boots, and a muscle shirt was working on a customer's arm. The sound of the carving tool echoed through the air.

"Can I help you?" he asked, not looking up from his paper. A cigarette hung from the corner of his mouth.

About 30 minutes later we were walking back downtown to the Expo site.

"So? Does it hurt? It looked painful. Lots of blood," Duane asked as we walked. "Let's take a look at it?"

I peel back the bloody cloth on my right arm to reveal my first tattoo. It reads "Harley" and it's in wings.

"Guess having no parents has its perks," Duane says.

That tattoo shop closed a long time ago now, maybe 20 years or more. I never went back there but over the years I acquired several more. One on my left arm is a cover up of a rebel cowboy with a skull; it's covered by a guardian angel with the words "With me." It's for my mother because she is with me always. On the other arm, I have several and a couple with words. "Tough times come and go, tough people last forever," " Hayden," and my first one:

"Harley." I have a Viking solider on my left forearm and a cross on my right forearm. One is for the adventurous part and the other for all the people I know who have passed, currently around 25. A tattoo on a person is a picture of themselves and the more you get, the bigger life map you have of yourself.

We eventually made it to the Expo site, but honestly we were quite stoned by that point. I went several times that summer and I don't recall much. But, those were good times, I guess.

The times I spent with my girlfriend were the best of times. Deanna came into my life and it became worth living for. Her warmth and innocence grounded me. She loved me for who I was. The very day after she graduated, she moved in with me. Shortly thereafter we headed to Edmonton where her mother, sister and two brothers lived. She missed her family and I would follow her anywhere. We started out with new beginnings, new surroundings, and the power of our love. We felt we could take on life head-on as long as we were together. Every single day we were together. After a year in Edmonton, we came back to BC, to the city of Kamloops where my brother was living at the time.

Five years went by with Deanna and I living together. We were engaged for a year. She was my life, and I hers. We had our issues like every other couple, but I constantly found myself battling my emotions. So many bottled up memories that oozed out of me usually when I was bombed, high and fucking wasted. I had a hunger for smashing my emotions and pushing them back down deep inside my body and mind. Cocaine and whiskey—Jack Daniel's—was a favourite mix during those days.

The local biker bars were my usual hang out. Hey! It's where I made my friends. Best place to find a job is hanging at the strip joints where the working guys hung out. But, sometimes a guy makes a few bucks dealing dope, collecting debts and you make your mark in the community. Every once in a while, some fuck face came by on a Friday night or something looking to square up a disagreement of friends with whom I may have interacted with. Perhaps a deal gone bad. The parking lot out back, 2:00 a.m. after the bar closes and people are gathering.

Bets, cash and hands wave in the air. I am shadow boxing off to the side. I take a swing and hit the metal door to the back of the bar.

"Kick his fucking ass, Henry! Terminator!" buddy is yelling in my face. He's slapping my back, "He has a glass jaw, you got this!"

"Come on, let's get this over with before the cops come," someone yells.

I pull out my paper flap, drop a line of cocaine on the dash of my car and roll up a fiver. With a big snort, the shit hits the top of my forehead and my nostrils burn. I feel a bead of sweat down the side of my head. I throw down one more line. *You can't fly on one wing* I say to myself as I lower my head and snort hard.

"Ready now!" I yell to the crowd. Cheers and hooting abound in the quiet night air. Deanna had no idea of my extra-curricular activities.

In 1990 home wasn't feeling like home. For me or Deanna. She had a job and had made really nice friends. But, Kamloops was a small town and sooner or later word gets around. Quickly, Deanna started questioning my actions and I knew things I was doing were wrong, but you make your choices and must accept the consequences. Seemed like our lives were escalating at a tremendous speed. I was clouded with my past, confused about my future, and wasted in the present. The biggest regret of my life and the worst emotional pain I would incur lasted for the next several years. Deanna and I came to an anguished decision to end our relationship. She moved back to where her father lived. I wouldn't see her again, ever. Broke my heart and I live with this forever.

In 2009 we connected on Facebook when I was living on Vancouver Island. We were planning on having a reunion when we could. She was married and had two children. It was our high school twenty-year reunion and I planned to come to Pitt Meadows in 2010.

We were chatting online and keeping in touch prior to the June reunion. But, we never met at the reunion. She passed away that March at age 39 from cancer. Same month as her birthday. Broke my heart again. I ended up visiting her that year but it was at the cemetery. I have never had a friend and lover so real. I've never even had a relationship last 5.8 years. It is a feeling of love a person unknowingly chases throughout their lives. I was in depression for years afterwards, I never truly recovered in my heart. I remember what it felt like when I was young and in love. You will never have that original true feeling of absolute love for another woman like you did for your first; it's a feeling deep in your heart. Those moments felt so real. Your arm around her shoulders, teasing words to trigger her emotions. Afterward showing her your endearing emotions with a peck on her cheek. Without a smirk or frown, you see her eyes looking into yours. Immediately her head falls onto your shoulder and her eyes close. You both are connecting and the warmth of each other's heartbeat is felt with the secureness of eternity. You kiss her one more time on her forehead. Feeling loved.

But, I have been taught how to distinguish between true feelings I have for someone else. As I get older I find myself alone most of the time. Relationships with women are real moments in time. The surreal emotions that a person goes through in such short periods of time makes us feel so alive.

The group of friends I grew up with in high schools in the country were the best thing that ever happened to me. Garibaldi and PMSS were the schools where I excelled the most. In socialism, alcoholism, drugs, fast cars and loose women. All before the age of 18. But, the acceptance and family feeling I received from my schoolmates was, by far, the best feeling I ever had. I made many mistakes those years and just barely stayed out of jail. Coming back and feeling the love from old friends truly meant that I had a life.

My oldest brother, Milan

My other brother, Tomas

My son Hayden in the year 2000 and I in Victoria

My Uncle Narcis and cousin Michelle in Australia

My sister Carmen and I in Peterborough, Ontario in 2018

My Mother and I

Duane, me and Danny year 2016

My son Hayden meeting my Father in Vancouver year 2016

My son Hayden and his two cousins Julie and Amanda

Jacqui Kaese my friend and owner of Spotlight Academy on Vancouver island

My buddy Phil and I in Victoria year 2019

Pic of me

My dad and I

My son and I

Deanna my high school love RIP

John RIP my buddy at the Rail

Me as a Catholic priest in the merry wives of Windsor year 2018

Me as a cop year 2017

Me dressed as an ugly woman

Working in Northern Alberta in 2018

Chapter 6 – Rock Creek

Gravel crunches under every step I take. I'm watching closely so as to not veer off course and roll down into the ditch. But looking up into the night sky. The stars are so vast and the sky is hypnotic as I walk steady along the highway. It's been three days since I left Kamloops. I had a drunken time in Vernon. The ride I had hitched dropped me off in front of a strip club in the centre of town. I was able to have a hamburger and fries and about six beers while watching the afternoon show. I talk lots to the girls, I always need some attention of some kind from a beautiful woman.

After a wash up in the washroom I stop in at the store for smokes. I roll up a joint for the road, crack a beer and put my thumb out. I found if you looked like a normal person who parties you'll get a quick pick up. And in no time a car pulls over. I down my beer and put the joint out, grab my bag and run up to the passenger side door.

I open the door and pop my head in "Thanks, man!"

"Kelowna, get in," the older guy who is driving shouts out as I am already getting comfy in the seat. One thing I taught myself is never let go of your stuff. My bag is on my lap just in case I need to exit a situation.

"You want a beer?" the driver asks me. He looks to be in his thirties, unshaven with messy hair. Dirty hands and jeans with a lunch box on the back seat. He probably finished work for the day and is heading home.

"Sure, thanks!" I reply.

He has the radio on to a channel with bad reception. Guess not much out here anyways. We pretty no where, nothing but road to follow. After not too long he pulls over and lets me out. I sling my duffle bag over my shoulder and it is starting to cool off after the sun sets. *Must be eleven-ish.* Feeling tired from the day's journey I give up on hitching for the day. *It's not like it used to be.* I figure another fifty or more kilometres till Rock Creek. Time to find a place to rest for the night. After about an hour I come across a rest area with some trees and bushes situated in a way that I can lie down and sleep without any worry. Plus, a good start in the morning and hopefully catch a ride the rest of the way. Before I realize it I am asleep.

I hate being woken up for a pee, especially when I am asleep and warm and comfy. The air is crisp with a layer of morning dew. The grass is moist as I put my hand down to push my way up. I take a few steps and unzip my pants. I relax a little and feel the warmth building up inside, and I pee. Aaaaaaaaa.

Not sure what time it is, the sun been up for a bit now. I figure six or seven o'clock. I light a cigarette and roll a joint. A little wake 'n bake is in order, again. I pull my Daytons off and let my feet air out. Crack open my last can of beer and halfway through my joint I think I am ready to hit the road. Beaverdell is not too far, I'll probably walk the way. Hopefully from there I can hook up a ride. I will check out the local bar when I get there. I don't have much money left so I hope I get to John's home soon. He said for me to stop in for a visit and he will help me out for a while. John was a shorter, lean, tattooed kind of guy with a smoke hanging off his yellow-stained fingers. He and my brother were good friends from way back and he lived in a log cabin in Rock Creek with his wife.

After several hours, I make it to the Beaverdell local pub. My feet and legs were tired and in need of rest. Counting my change and what paper I had left, there is enough for a burger and a beer. THANK YOU. There are four people in here: the bartender, the cook and some guy in his eighties at a table having a beer and cigarette. I bet he has not left since the bar opened the first day. I am the fourth person here, I guess no ride here for me. I eat up and get walking the highway because I am not staying here broke. Probably what happened to that old guy at the table.

I make my way to Hwy 33 on the edge of town and continue walking. Every so often a car comes by and my thumb goes out. I'm thirsty and my feet are sore. I'm constantly thinking of Deanna. Oh my God I miss her so very much. I wish there was a way to fix our love, but I screwed up too many times. I feel so lost and alone and I start to cry. Yet, I walk more, I hear gravel crunching and tires stopping suddenly as I look up. Drying my eyes with my hand I see the pick-up truck pulling over. Buddy slams into reverse and he brakes a few feet in front of me. I walk over to the passenger side door and I see a gorgeous blonde with a pink top and cut off shorts. She has a yellow hair clip in her long curly hair.

"Where you headed?" she asks.

"The pub in Rock Creek would be great!" I reply.

The older dude driving is a red neck hippie guy with a ripped up jean vest and cut off shorts.

"Hop in! Slide over baby and let the guy in," he says to the gorgeous blonde. She opens the door to let me in.

"You smoke pot?" she asks as she passes me a reefer. I jump in and close the door as I grab the joint. An hour later they drop me off at the Rock Creek Pub.

"Thanks!" I say waving them off. I would have a couple of beers and wait for John to come pick me up.

I spent the next several weeks living and working at John's place with his wife, Ann. They were cool older folks who worked and grew vegetables at home. They helped me out and fed me as a favour to my brother, Tomas. I needed time to get my head together and I couldn't smoke enough or drink enough to forget. It was all too fresh and my love was like no other.

I hung out at the pub with John a couple days of the week, and then one day I met a fella. He says he was leaving his job as a farm hand and they were looking for a replacement. Just a few miles down the highway from John's place was the Cuthbertson's Farm, one of the largest hay farms in the territory. Bruce was the head of the family. I did odd chores, irrigation lines, tractor work, hay bailing and stacking and in return I had a 600 sq ft cabin right on the Rock Creek, $1000 a month cash plus I had lunch with the family every day. I always had it in me for hard work and I needed the money. But my thoughts were tearing me up every day.

In my little cabin by the creek I had a small black and white TV with rabbit ears and I could only get the CBC with half ass reception. My ghetto blaster was fine, it was just the area. No radio stations were anywhere close by. Every so often I could hear some favourite songs come on and I would fiddle with the wires and tuner trying to improve the reception. But, whenever any Meatloaf songs came on—I don't know but the songs soothed my soul. So much so that I convinced myself that I had to have the cassette *Bat Out of Hell*.

I would work on the farm till lunch, meet at the main house and eat with the family, and get new orders for the afternoon. Most of my mornings consisted of walking the fields and switching the irrigation lines and watering the hay fields. Songs from Meatloaf's radio songs churned in my head and thoughts of my recent past plagued my days. I needed the cassette to heal, and I decided to head back to Kamloops to find it.

After searching throughout the Kamloops new and used tape stores I couldn't find one single Meatloaf tape. Damn it! It was my last night in town and I had no place to stay. The previous night, I crashed at a friend's place. Tonight, I went to my old drinking hole, The Thompson Inn, and had a bite to eat and proceeded to drink some beers. As the night went on I found myself at a table with a few new friends I made. By 2:00 a.m. I am stumbling out with a lady. She took me back to her place, trailer court on the other side of town. We proceeded to drink and screw till morning at which time she says, "I guess you should leave now, my husband will be home from work soon."

I am in shock. "WHAT?" I say as I am now quickly getting my clothes on. "Fuck Woman! What the hell!"

I start cursing in my wiped out state. Leaving and closing the screen door I walk quickly while lighting up a smoke. I would head back the farm in Rock Creek.

A couple days later I was walking the fields and switching the irrigation lines. I finished the first field, which usually takes about twenty minutes or so first thing in the morning. The first field is next to Hwy 33 and the second field is on the other side of the highway. The next farm in either direction is a few clicks away as well. So, before I cross the road I usually roll a homey for the road. Toss the roach in the bag and I cross the two lane highway. As I walk across I can see something on the gravel shoulder on the other side. As I step closer I can see that it is a cassette. It is! And immediately I see Meatloaf *Bat Out of Hell* labels on it.

Are you kidding me? There is no way it works. What are the chances? Someone must have thrown it out the window of their car. But, how is it here? Right where I cross?

I immediately did the rest of my chores and skipped lunch with the family. I went to my cabin and put it in my ghetto, pressed play and prayed, *dear God just this little thing to make me happy please?*

Worked like it was new! For whatever reason I immediately started healing. I totally believe that I have a guardian angel looking after me and its my dear Uncle Narcis. I still missed my Deanna immensely but now I could get by a little bit more. I listened to that tape over and over and over for weeks. I still have it to this day and I will never forget you Deanna, Amen

I would spend the rest of the summer working on the farm. I'd sometimes tube ride the Rock Creek from the foot of my cabin door the whole way down river to the local pub. There I'd hang out with the locals and catch a ride home at closing time. I found out a few months later that Mr. Cuthbertson died when a logging truck lost its load on a corner of a steep highway. Rest in peace sir, and thank you for your kindness.

I had kept in touch with my mother after she was released awhile back. She was starting over again. She was a beauty in her younger years, but as the years went by her beautiful red hair turned more gray and she battled her weight just as much her mental health. But, she was always strong this way, so much resiliency to life, always with a smile. I cannot count how many times she started over with her belongings. She collected a lot of stuff and all the walls of her apartment were covered with pictures. As long as she took her meds she handled life like a normal person. It was when she stopped taking them that her life was turned upside down. She was diagnosed with paranoid delusional schizophrenia. My mother had it rough but she always bounced back. She loved me and her family and we would call each other every Sunday and talk. I miss that and have not experienced such love since her.

She loved her family, friends and the men that came into her life. Cigarettes, wine, good food with a social game of cards with her friends on the weekends gave her a little bit of sunshine on days that were mostly dark.

At one point she was living in Victoria with her boyfriend of a year or so, Lubomir. He was a short, stalky, well-kept kind of guy with a puffy mustache. He was a tough Czech who bragged about his mandatory stint in the Czech Army in his younger years. He took care of her, and me and my brothers appreciate it. I missed my mom and I decided to see her on my way to Victoria on Vancouver Island. Her and Lubomir were employed as caretakers for the Skyline Motel, a small, clean motel just on the edge of downtown.

After several days of hitch-hiking, walking for kilometres, sleeping on park benches, church steps, under a tree or in a bush and in bus stations, I would take a welfare cheque when I could. Even a bus pass and few food stamps for the local shelter in order to keep going. I found my way to Victoria in the beginning of fall, 1991. My mother snuck me into the storage room in the motel at night for me to sleep for several nights. During the days, I was in search of any kind of work. And, like I said before, the best place to meet someone is in the local bar.

Chapter 7 – The Brass Rail

The Colony Motor Inn was a hotel built on Douglas Street in Victoria around 1965. The Sandman Inn is now there with The Shark Club attached. The Colony had the Brass Rail, which operated as a strip joint during the day and a rock club at night. It was just down the street from The Skyline Motel where my mother worked for a while before moving back to East Vancouver. John, six-foot-six with a blonde mane of and a mustache to match, was the head doorman at The Brass Rail. Long and lanky, he wore biker rings with skulls on his massive fingers.

"Like brass knuckles, they leave damage behind when I punch someone in the head," he told me.

His wallet was a big piece of leather attached to a chain that was hooked to his belt. He took no shit from no one and scared the shit right out of you when he got mad. We connected right away, I think partially because I was not scared of him. I stand my ground and in turn earn the respect and thus we knew we could depend on each other when things got bad.

And they would, as bad as it could ever come.

Think of rock stars, drug dealers, bullies, Casanovas, bodyguards, bouncers all rolled into one. That was John and I and the rest of the patrons who came to this place. We called The Colony Motor Inn and The Brass Rail our home. This was the right place for me!

I quickly got to know John and the rest of the staff at the hotel and landed myself a job there. John showed me everything about dealing with drunks, keeping the staff safe and working with our local drug dealers. Soon he introduced me to his friends and before long he and I started dealing cocaine and marijuana to clientele in the bar and hotel.

"One for me and one for you," I would say to John as I chopped up a couple of lines on the toilet lid in the staff bathroom.

"Oh yeah, this batch is killer," he said as he rolls up a twenty dollar bill and snorts the massive line. Now let's get rid of this ounce bag and we can get an eight ball for ourselves, plus some more through the night."

Soon I had a piece of leather attached to my belt with a chain and it was full of bills and flaps. I wouldn't sleep much for two, three, maybe four days at a time from working at the bar till three. Already wasted, we continued with the after parties and side gigs (collecting or security for our employers) to acquire just enough cocaine to freebase with for as long as we possibly could.

I wanted to belong and be loved by my new friends. John, this tall, good looking biker tough guy lived with his girlfriend, Jill, a voluptuous brunette, and quiet mommy-girl type. They lived in a two-bedroom apartment on Inverness Street in Victoria and would have me over sometimes for dinner before we headed for work in the evening. For the last month I had not been staying at my mom's place, she was starting to get heat from her employer so

I exited. I managed to sneak into the UHAUL lockers each night before they closed. It was heated, quiet and safe. I brought a cooler with ice and beer and bread, cigarettes and a bottle to pee in. I would leave as soon as they reopened the next morning.

Jill moved out one day and I asked John if he wanted a roommate. And he most certainly did, he was behind in rent and my welfare cheque would cover it. I moved in right away. Jill was taking all her stuff, which meant John was left with nothing. And I had nothing. But, the building next door had a fire, and someone's belongings were inside. One night after our shifts at about four in the morning, higher than a fucking kite, a fidgety stroll next door. We grabbed the couch, tables, chairs, forks and knives. That's how John and I started our 20-year relationship till his death (I will tell you about that soon). We became two of the toughest, meanest guys in our hood and at the bar/hotel for the next few years.

The Colony Motor Inn had a restaurant downstairs, the night club/strip joint on the main, a pool, a weight room, a car wash, and about a hundred rooms over three floors. In a regular shift the doormen would take turns throughout the night doing the rounds of the hotel and property. We had keys for all the doors and responded to guest's complaints. After only being there a few weeks I quickly earned the respect of the bar staff and the management.

This one Thursday night the hotel front desk received a few complaints of a couple women kissing in the pool and I was asked to check it out.

"Hello ladies, excuse me!" I said to the two naked women in the pool.

"Hi there, you're kind of cute. Are you hotel security?" one of the ladies asked me.

Both women were beautiful and they were embracing in the shallow end of the pool. A couple beers were on the deck close to them. One of them stood up and climbed out of the pool. She walked over and I saw she had no swim suit on at all. She put her arms around me and pulled me in close. I enjoyed the embrace while our eyes locked. Her right hand dropped down to my crotch and she started rubbing me.

"Ummm, you're not allowed to be in here naked, you know. We are receiving complaints?"Why don't you two take the party to your room and I will clean up these beers for you?" I picked up their two beer cans.

"Aaahh c'mon, give us a break and come in and join us?" the other gorgeous blonde said to me. She French kissed the other girl.

A crackling sound erupted from my hand-held two way radio.

"Henry, how goes it? What's going on in the pool?" It was John on the other end from the front door of The Rail. "Doors are open and people are here; I need a hand."

I looked down at the girls as I threw the beer cans in the trash and clicked the button on the mic.

"I am on my way! I'm just kicking two strippers out of the pool."

I helped the ladies out of the pool and handed them their towels. "We are having a big band tonight, you coming?" I asked them. "Come before ten and I'll let you in. It's Helix, the band! You two want to party after? I can bring the party favours?"

They looked at me with towels just barely wrapped around their bodies, "Yes! That sounds great! We love that band, and you will come back with us after," they said as they giggled their way out.

I walked them to the elevator and gave one of them a small folded up piece of paper. I slapped the other's towel-covered ass. The doors of the elevator closed and go up while I headed down the hallway to the restroom. Usually no one used this restroom so it was a safe place to pinch a line. I scraped a bit off the flap and onto the counter, grabbed another flap and did the same till I had a nice big line. I put them in my pocket and grabbed a dollar bill from my wallet. I rolled it up and put one end deep in my nostril and the other to the start of the line and away we snort it all up!

"Yeah baby!" I say.

I wiped down the counter with my two fingers, picked up the remnants and rubbed my gums with them. I checked myself in the mirror and took a piss. *Let's get it on,* I think, as I head down the hallway popping a cigarette into my mouth. I lit it while scanning the crowd.

The bar was getting busy quickly this Saturday night with Helix playing. I walked through the bar passing by our regulars and the waitresses.

"Hey Candy! Let me help you there," as I grabbed a few dirty glasses off the table she was cleaning up.

"Thanks! Henry, if you need more you know where to go!" she replied. Candy was her nickname for a reason.

"Hey, here I am if you want to take a break?" I said to John as I stepped up beside his six-foot-six slender frame. He combs his long blonde hair and adjusts his neatly ironed white collared shirt and black tie. He was enjoying himself and checking a young girl's i.d.

"Sounds great, Hank! *I'll be back!*" he said, laughing. They all thought I looked like Arnold Schwarzenegger.

"It's ten bucks cover tonight," I said to the next group of customers who are all intoxicated. But, who am I to judge? John and I drank a twixer of vodka in like two drinks each in the park across the street before our shift. It's what we did almost every night we were there, which was five or six days a week. Plus, if we had some it wasn't unusual to fire up a pop can—as we were usually running out of cigarettes—before heading to the liquor store.

"How you guys doing? Go right in, enjoy the night," I said to eight Hell's Angels that usually came when the good bands or hot strippers were in town. They left their bikes outside where we could keep our eyes on them while working the door. It's always good practice to know who to please and who you can be the biggest asshole to. Like the next three guys.

"Hold up, fifteen bucks to get in." I had my hand up to this guy's face, looking square into his eyes. "Fifteen bucks," I say again.

The tall handsome fella with a mohawk was caught off guard as he looked up at me. "What? For the three of us, right?" he said, stepping back from my hand.

I shake my head. "Each," I said.

"What the fuck, man. It says ten at the door!" he replied.

I looked at his two friends, and they both took two steps back. "You want in? Fifteen bucks each, cause it's getting full inside. We are near max," I told them.

"Its eight o'clock! It's not full yet—what bullshit you talking about?" the guy behind yelled in a scratching catlike meow.

"In or not? People behind you, now yes or no?" I stood firm and solid.

"Pay him, Jim. He is the front guy," said the short one in the back.

The three of them paid me, I stamped their palms and they entered, talking under their breath. I just counted the cash and put fifteen bucks in my pocket. "Next!" I said to the young ladies in line. "How you doing gorgeous? Go right in. I will be in shortly to buy you a drink. What's your name?" I asked the tall, gorgeous blonde with legs that went to heaven.

"Marie, what's yours?" she replied.

"Henry. I will be by shortly," I said to her. "Next!"

Another doorman took the door and I took a walk around the hotel parking lot. Looking for shit to happen, coke customers, passed out drunks. My own dealers were usually sitting in their cars with hot women doing lines off the dash. We would escort the drunks off the property.

"Stop it!!! Please stop!!" A woman was screaming out with her hands covering her face.

"Oh my god!! Stop, stop!! Oh my God!!" another woman yelled.

I walked around the corner to see a small crowd watching in horror. One man was on the ground out cold while another man was standing above him. The white guy out cold was unrecognizable with all the blood upon his face, the other guy was dressed in Dayton boots and jeans with a leather jacket. He picked the limp body up and pulled him to the curb of the street and dropped his head on the top of the curb.

"No please stop it!! Enough! Stop!!"

People were gathering and screaming. I made my way through the crowd just in time to see the guy on the ground get his jaw broken was a boot is thrust down on his head.

Just as I confronted stomping man, the police and an ambulance arrived. Lights, sirens and people intoxicated all around. The cops arrested the stomper and took him away.

Just then John came by. "You OK, Henry? What the fuck happened? Write a report before you forget and quickly. We need you inside. It's getting fucking busy and it's welfare Wednesday weekend. Go pinch a line and pull yourself together and see you inside."

I went downstairs to the front desk to write my report but after I hit the staff bathroom for a pick-me-up. Just as I finished in the bathroom a call from Stephen, the assistant bar manager, came through the hand held radio. Stephen was this older short guy who looked like a pit bull. "Henry! You here? Need you in the bar right away! Henry you there?"

I answered Stephen promptly and headed to the bar upstairs. John came through the rear end of the nightclub where Helix was playing their first set. People everywhere, the room was packed solid. Smoke in the air, a cigarette in my mouth, I adjusted my clip-on tie, threw my shoulders back, chin up. With one last wipe of my nose I pushed my way through the crowd.

The stage was to the west of the bar at the south end of the building. I came in from the north corner close to the stage. Music was its normal ear-shattering loudness. Some doormen wore earplugs but I didn't care for them myself. I made my round about the room checking out everyone and looking for Stephen and John. I saw them by the pool tables in the east corner but I came across a table of gorgeous chicks first.

"Marie, how are you? What are you drinking? I have to get going we are super busy but I will stop by again, ok?" I asked her. She nodded with a smile and was quickly distracted by her friends, giggling away.

I made my round to the restroom and went inside to check it out. It was on my way to the pool tables and I just couldn't walk by without going in the shitters. It was usually an easy way to confiscate someone's dope and kick them out on their ass. I quietly stepped onto a toilet next to a stall where I saw someone is inside. I popped my head over the wall to see a guy pretending to be on the crapper but is actually chopping up a line on the toilet roll. I quietly stepped back down off the toilet and stood in front of his stall and then I burst open the door. The guy was surprised and off guard. I grabbed his flap off the toilet roll and told him to scram. I grabbed him and helped him to his feet, put the flap in my pocket and escorted the guy out past the pool tables. Stephen the "pit bull" and John were standing at the front entrance and I aggressively manhandle the guy by the scruff of the neck out the door and past the other doorman.

"See you next weekend!" I told the guy as he was straightening out his shirt and pants and walking away.

"So? What's going on?" I asked Stephen.

"Another one in the can huh?" he said to me.

We all scanned the crowd constantly and set a game plan for this super volatile evening with over 200 people. It was standing room only. John looked over at me and winked.

"They never learn do they, John?" I replied.

"Nope and it's what keeps us busy. Now keep your eyes on the three tables front row of the dance floor. Deedee told me the couple of guys are jerks but there seems to be seven or so in the group."

Deedee was our go to waitress. She was a biker chic with a biker boyfriend. Short brown hair, late twenties and looked in her thirties but kept a great figure. Hell of a waitress.

Stephen tapped me on the shoulder and said, "Henry, I want you down on the other side of the bar so you can watch the dance floor, OK?"

I nodded and made my way through the crowd, saying hi to the bar staff and waitresses as they walked by me. I'd never seen it so busy. It was unbelievable. I pulled out a cigarette, lit it and leaned on the bar looking at the people in front of me. The band was on stage. Deedee was carrying her tray full of drinks over to the group that were being disruptive when the glasses fell off the tray and crashed all over the floor.

"What the fuck! You asshole! You tripped me!" Deedee was screaming at the same guy who I made pay extra at the door earlier. And Deedee was one girl you didn't want to mess with either, let me tell you. Any other time we had issues with the female gender, Deedee was our go to person. She didn't hesitate to throw punches. She looked over at me as I ran towards her and grabbed the guy by the shoulders.

All his buddies decided that no one was leaving. They kept saying that they paid their cover and it's the waitress who is being the bitch. Within a blink of my eye I am hit in the back by a chair and I thrust onto the floor. The next thing I knew the whole fucking bar was rioting just like an old Burt Reynolds bar fight. Everyone—and I mean everyone—was part of this massive fight. Chairs, glasses and tables were being thrown or used as a weapon. Women were jumping on men's backs, screaming and hitting.

"Get everyone outside, Henry! The cops are on the way! Everyone outside now!!"

John grabbed people and pulled them to the front doors. I looked across the room to see the Hell's Angels keeping their own and making their way out. They didn't want any unwanted publicity, that's for sure.

"Look out!!" a woman by the pool tables screamed. A very loud smash exploded in the bar as the front window was broken by a chair.

Tables were thrown over and people were being thrown over the tables. Chairs were flying everywhere and the sounds of bottles and glasses breaking was in the air. The band stopped playing. They looked to get off the stage but there was nowhere to go. During the day, the strippers used the same stage and walked to it from the side door that went to the hotel. Everywhere, people were fighting and blocking their way. We had six doormen and I saw them all in scuffles, bleeding all over their white shirts. I grabbed someone and brought them outside as the paddy wagon and police showed up. By then, more than half the patrons were outside fighting, which was fine. Just as long as they were out of the bar.

That was the biggest bar brawl I have ever been but it would not be my last. Over the next dozen years, I worked half a dozen different hotels, bars or night clubs on the island or in Australia. I dealt with Asian gangs a lot, Russian gangs, welfare recipients and drug addicts, want-to-be bikers and drunk women. This was normal for me. And I taught myself how to deal with circumstances, remain patient and use force only if absolutely necessary. I've been stabbed, had guns pointed at me, been beat up, in some scary shit and showdowns. Usually the gang or people would wait outside for the bar to close and try to get me. I was always looking over my shoulder, and I usually carried a knife. You just never know. I learned that early on while in Victoria. I have broken every finger and dislocated my thumbs fighting. I have many scars on my knuckles from teeth and/or fingernails. I have woken in the hospital and sent plenty of men there. Many stories I can tell just doing security. And not all are bad either! I met lots of beautiful people that I loved.

In the second summer working at The Rail I was slowly moving on from the thoughts of Deanna, though if she was there I would have been a grateful man. But, I wouldn't hear from her for another twenty years. I knew the bar and selling drugs and fucking women was about the best time in my whole life. That summer I had an endless supply of women, hot tubs, parks, cars, bathrooms, pavement, grass or on the beaches around town. Over forty that summer, in three months. Cocaine and all the perks, I felt like a rock star. But better, I was security for every band that came to play at The Rail. I was the guy with access to anything in the hotel and John was leading the way for the two of us.

We were connected with a few guys in town and selling cocaine, moving and doing. Kicking johns out of hotel rooms late into the nights and early into sunrise. A hooker would call her pimp that she was having trouble and the pimp would call our guy. In turn, he called John and I to go deal with the issues. Just like Bruce Willis and Samuel L. Jackson in *Pulp Fiction*. Or we were muscle for some piece of shit that couldn't pay his bill. I'd walk out of an apartment with a stereo or television. Or just yank the necklace off some guy's neck for payment. We were always out and about in Victoria throughout the nights and sleeping the days.

It was six o'clock in the morning and I left Helix's room and went downstairs to the front desk. Chris the deejay was supposed to meet me. He was a player in his DJ booth—always women around him. We both had bracelets on our wrists in order to buy Guns 'n Roses, Faith No More, and Metallica tickets early.

"Morning, Stew. How goes it this morning?" I asked.

Stew was our front desk graveyard shift person. Glasses on, pens in the shirt pocket of his long-sleeved company shirt, he was usually on the computer playing games. I leaned up on the counter in order to gain my balance. I had been wasted since hitting the pipe the day before at two in the afternoon before heading to work. I had partied with Helix after the bar brawl till now. I hadn't stopped. The telephone rang and Stew answered. With a disbelieving look he told me to head up to the bar manager's room, 215.

"I have to call an ambulance, Henry! Go up there and see what's up. There is a woman on the phone and she is hard to understand because she is so hysterical."

Chris met me at the door to the manager's room. I knocked loudly. The door opened and an older woman came into the hall. She was hysterical and said, "I think he is dead?"

I told Chris to tell Stew what happened and make sure an ambulance is on its way. Dan was our bar manager, he was in his forties, a big heavy-set man who smoked three packs of cigarettes a day. It was nothing for him to carry three packs in his shirt pockets. He had one lung removed, or that's what we heard. But, there he was, naked on the bed in the hotel room, still absolutely still. Heart attack was my first thought, and I had taken a CPR course through my new day job not too long before. I jumped up on the bed beside him and frantically started to apply chest compression, periodically checking his pulse and breathing. There was none I could find so I gave him mouth-to-mouth. It seemed like forever before the paramedics showed up and took over. But, it was too late; he passed.

This took me over the top with emotions. The year was already full of the deaths of people I knew, about seven by then and it was only August. And there were more to come. Seemed to be so much heartache in my life and I tried really hard to stay wasted, drunk and stoned because it was the only way I knew to cope. Usually people I confided in were friends or acquaintances. Sometimes it was hard to figure shit out, or get any answers to the many questions like, Why? Why did this person die? Why did people do certain shit in the bars and to other people? Life was all about surviving and making it to the next day. Using drugs and alcohol made life much more manageable. I was having way too much fun, but I was also getting by slowly. I somehow felt I'd be OK. I started looking for a real, steady, normal job—not washing dishes or at the bars. The Colony Motor Inn and The Brass Rail closed down in 1993.

Soon after putting the word out to my friends, I had a lead. I handed out my resume, which wasn't much of one; a few companies for labour work in the construction industry. The natural gas distribution sector was exploding on the south island. One afternoon I was hanging with my friend Brad, his three kids and his wife, Lana, in their townhouse on Blanshard Street. Brad was putting the finishing touches on his eighteen-foot outboard boat.

"She is ready to go, Henry, why don't you come with me and Cody?" he said. Cody was his three year old son, and that kid had character, I tell you. Like, he knew he was gorgeous already and every female that saw him commented on his long blonde hair and ocean blue eyes. Brad was in his late twenties. Selling weed made him more cash than having a minimum wage job, but doing both, he made a comfortable home for his family. He worked part time at a convenience store as well. Brad and Lana both loved tattoos and their kids; they were my closest friends at the time.

"I'm in! I'd love to go fishing, Brad, thanks!" I replied.

"We will leave early, OK, like seven. We will go off the Sooke basin," he said.

I nod and shake hands with him and leave for home.

The next morning I was up at six thirty and quietly got myself organized while John was sleeping in his room. Brad lived but a few blocks away from me so I would leave shortly. As I was closing the door to the apartment, the phone rang. I figured it was Brad calling to cancel the trip for some reason, so I ran inside to answer the phone.

"Hello?"

"Is this Henry? You applied for a job here the other day?" he said.

"Yes, I am."

I am kind of excited for what he is about to say because I was hoping to get a full-time job. With so many people and friends dying this year I didn't want to be next. I was ready to change and do something more with my life. I just needed a chance to prove myself.

"You want a job? We need someone ASAP, right now, today!" the fella on the other end was very anxious about an answer.

"Yes sir, I can be in right away, thank you."

I hung up with him, quickly dialed Brad and explained my opportunity. He knew I was looking for a job, it just happened on the day of the inauguration of his boat.

"Good luck, Henry. Stop by after and tell me how it went. Plus, I will have a fish here for you for dinner tonight. I have another guy I can call to come with me and Cody. Good luck!" he said.

I hang up, put a different set of clothes on and head out. Into the elevator down the hall and on my mountain bike to my new job as a labourer with the gas company. I was pumped.

I was all exhausted after my first day and searching for a beer. I hit the liquor store and made my way to Brad and Lana's to tell them about my day and hear his fishing stories. Upon arriving to his place I noticed his car was not in the driveway, nor his boat and trailer. I knocked and Lana opened the door. She was crying and people in the living room were all crying and hugging each other.

"Henry! I am so glad you're here. Brad and Cody and the friend he picked up never made it!"

I was totally in disbelief and I broke down. "What happened?"

Lana was too traumatized to tell me so another person says that the three of them went out in the Sooke basin fishing, all with life jackets on, but they were found miles from each other drowned in the ocean. No explanation of why. Their boat was ripped in pieces and Search and Rescue retrieved them.

I thought about how close my apartment door was from being closed and me going down the elevator. A few more minutes and I would not have heard the phone ring.

Just before I gave my notice at the bar, I had started dating Marie. She had beautiful long legs, and was a very attractive lady who worked in an office. She had long blonde hair and fingernails to match. She dressed very well in business attire and smelled like a blossoming flower; I felt very fortunate. We quickly bonded and within three months I moved in with her.

John was going to move in with his steady lady now, too. Michele was a small, short woman with long brown hair and green eyes. They looked happy, this tall, tough good looking guy and his tiny cute gal.

Marie and I had a lot in common; we played cards and enjoyed each other's company. Things were steamy for the next three years. I rented my first house with her; she was a great influence on me though we seemed to fight constantly. I was dealing with my use of crack and cocaine, though drinking was probably my biggest problem. Start with a few drinks and then the cravings started, then the lines. I hide my pleasures like a true addict. Our relationship came to an end slowly over a period of time, but we still remained good friends.

I wanted to change, I knew there was a better life. There had to be a damn good reason why I hadn't died yet like so many others that shouldn't have. With a growing list of charges and a pending court date I knew there was a good chance I would go to jail. Deep inside, I knew that was not the road for me. So, I went to the local recruiter for the Armed Forces. I needed discipline, a path, a reason to live a good life. I needed to get off the cocaine for good. I would join the army if that's what it took for me to turn around. I had an interview and told my story to the recruiter. With a letter from the recruiter I was able to stay out of jail, and it would be the last time I ever did anything illegal again. Even though I wasn't accepted into the Forces I decided that I needed to help myself.

I started by achieving my GED and concentrating on the construction job I had. I used my strength to outwork everyone around me. I set the example for myself and pushed for the attention of others to show that I had something they didn't. A reason to live for greatness. Picks, shovels, pry bars, track shovels were my drugs. I dug ditches and installed residential gas lines. I was determined to change, to prove to myself that I had a purpose.

But, I had money problems. I declared bankruptcy. My past party days and excessive drug use caused me to take advantage of the employment insurance benefits and they were being garnisheed from my wages. This financial crisis put a huge strain on my relationship with Marie.

Our first date was on Valentine's Day 1993 and we ended our relationship on Valentine's Day 1996. But, not before I found out my best friend was moving in with her just a few weeks later. He had been my friend me since the first day we all met. Son of a bitch! Funny thing is I played flag football with this ex-friend and he felt my wrath on the field the rest of season. He ended up quitting. I never saw him again, thank you. But Marie? Well, we been keeping a beautiful friendship and we keep in touch. Hell—she still has those legs!

I was renting my very own place and working hard in the trenches all over the south island for the gas company. I had a pick-up truck and I found myself a puppy. Going into Glenwood Meats in Langford, I saw a sign: "Puppies for sale." They were German shepherd crossed with wolf—little puppies, they were awesome.

Out of the young litter there was one that was out of the group. She was happy to see me, like the rest, but she knew to hang back. The runt, they say. I named her Zoe. I walked her every day and took her to dog school to learn hand commands together. I even took her to work with me in the pick-up every day. We were inseparable. I loved her and needed her, heck we needed each other. She had great big floppy ears that were too big for her head but her flaws, I felt, complemented my own.

I continued to work hard, and I knew in order to achieve something great I had to push myself. I started bugging the backhoe operator at lunchtimes to teach me more. Every lunch break while the operator ate, I would jump in the machine and just play with the controls and buttons. Slowly over time I began driving and operating and learning how to dig ditches. Not by shovel and picks but by hydraulics. And Zoe would be in my pick-up sitting in the back on nice summer days, watching me. Every chance I had I would bring her a hug and treats.

I found new friends on the football fields all over the island as well. I never had the opportunity to play sports when I was younger, so I embraced the Island Flag Football League. Before I knew it, my new cravings for a high came on the fields throwing the football. I had stopped using cocaine for good, on my own, and I felt like I had a meaning now to live. In November 1995 I played for The Killer Bees football team. We travelled up to the north island to a small logging, fishing town named Campbell River for the BC tournament. Our team was a great fun bunch of guys who took over a whole floor of a hotel for the long weekend tournament.

The weekend was an absolute animal house, genuinely just like the movie. In the movie there was the pool scene with the chocolate bar, but at our hotel in the hot tub was an actual piece of poo. Let's say there was not much sleeping going on. In the tournament we made the final playoff game, which we very nearly missed! Our entire team partied all night long in the bar in Campbell River, and I met a very beautiful young waitress. The next morning we all slept in and when we made it to the ballpark, the referee was a minute away from forfeiting our whole team! So, without any warmups, stretches, or even a moment to spare, we started the final playoff game. Having beers to get through, we actually won by one point against a team that had not lost in years! We pulled it off! We were BC Champions!

That night we went back to the bar, Sgt. O'Flaherty's at the Coast Hotel, where I met a beautiful, petite, older waitress with long curly brown hair, and a smile that made me melt. She was hung over from the night before as well. I couldn't stop thinking of her and took every chance I could to see her. The team and I had to leave the next day back to Victoria, but I swore to her I would be back. As a few months went by with several hundred calls, I found my way back to this small fishing town to be with the woman I fell in love with.

Chapter 8 – Somewhere in 1994

Campbell River was a long drive from Victoria. Taking the old island highway as it wound along the eastern coastline, I would stop periodically to let Zoe out for a pee. She lay in her bed under the canopy in the back of my old black 1977 Ford half ton pickup. She was used to her second home in the pickup, as she came to work with me every day. It had been three and half years since I received the phone call to start my job, the day my friends died fishing, and I was looking for a new life. I had to take the chance of a new beginning for us in a new town. I had my belongings in the back with Zoe.

As I drove the long winding highway up island, the traffic was single lane and bumper to bumper. My old truck had some issues that I tried to stay on top of by always having tools and spare parts on hand. I had the stereo pumping, beer cracked and I lit a joint for the road with my Zippo. I wanted to get up there as soon as I could because I was so excited to be with this beautiful woman and start working toward the future I desired. Seeing some friends and their families happy made me long for a a normal life. It was something I was envious of since my mother first fell ill and I went to foster care.

Almost five and half hours later I arrived to Jo's address. It was raining and dark gray outside. As soon as she opened the door, the clouds broke and rays of sunshine fell upon her beautiful face.

"Hi! I'm here!" I said.

"C'mon in, how was the drive?" she asked. "Come meet my son, Dustin!! Come say hi!"

Footsteps pounded down the stairs, and a young boy with curly brown hair came bounding down to greet me. He was about seven.

"Meet my dog, Zoe," I told them as I opened the canopy at the back of the truck. That was the introduction to my new family and I couldn't wait to start loving and embracing them.

It was a honeymoon-type beginning for us, as there was a lot of passion and we bonded quickly; it didn't last too long though. And perhaps in hind sight, following my gut instinct instead of my heart and her gorgeous ass things could have been different. But, as it went we had a wonderful son, Hayden. There is nothing I ever wanted in my life more than a child of my own. I knew I had the love, compassion and outright desire to mentor and be someone to another person that I never had.

But, before Hayden's birth I had to adjust to Dustin. Unfortunately, he was going through the exact same shit. No father around to hug. I put myself there for him and for the future of us all. Dusty was a very confused, angry and sad boy who had attention deficit problems. Had major issues with school and authority. And it didn't help much that his mother was in the beginning phases of a break up with a previous boyfriend. She reminded me in way of my mother. Her ex-boyfriend would hit her, intimidate and who knows what else. This had a tremendous effect on her mentally and she was very timid about men in general. I could only reassure her that I never would become physical and instead wanted to protect her.

She let me into her life and I let her into mine. We spent every day together falling in love. we both know just how hard it can get when you decide you want to change things in your life. I wouldn't hear from her for several days and I had to be responsible for Dusty, which tested our relationship mightily. I would find out she had fallen off the wagon—and in a big way—for several days. At times, it was so tough that I just wanted to leave, go back to Victoria and forget about this. But, I could not leave Dusty by himself; poor kid had gone through so much before, and was just coming around socially. Furious as I was, I truly felt that she and I needed each other. She showed up one afternoon and in great apologetic sorrow. I knew exactly what kicking the habit was like and I was not going to let the drugs win. We both worked on kicking our drug habits, and we started to concentrate on us. Slowly day-by-day, we got better for each other. After a year, I went to her father and asked for his blessing.

A few months later she was pregnant. We were so thrilled to have each other and the opportunity for our family with Dustin. we rented a house, painted a baby room, hung out together every day, every moment. I think she was most beautiful at seven months pregnant on our day trip to the Jaun de Fuca beach, trips we went on several times together. Slowly, we dropped our old crutches.

I ended up working for ten days in a camp on the Knight Inlet. I took a float plane to the mainland, then to a small bay. Hayden Bay is its name. Established sometime in mid 1800s, it once had a full community that traded with the coast natives of the time. There was logging, fishing, gold mines, hunting and anything to trade and sell or live on. We were crabbing, catching prawns, fishing salmon everyday I was there. It was a most beautiful place to me, and the name Hayden was just as nice. Jo agreed, and when our son was born there was nothing else to call him but Hayden. Jo underwent over twenty five hours of labour till they had to do the big c. I was the happiest ever in my life holding my baby boy in my arms. With my older brother, Tomas, beside me I finally felt like a man should.

Soon the pressure of family started to be overwhelming. I never truly made any friends in this new town and having little experience I found myself constantly searching for work. Being such a small town as well was frustrating for me most times. Seems I couldn't go anywhere without Jo finding out by her friends spotting me whether I was sitting in my truck on the edge of town or in the local bar. She had been there her whole life and knew everyone! I became insecure, paranoid, defensive and guarded towards her friends. Over the next 15 months our relationship became strained by my attitude and her insecurities of men combined with my lack of money and too many bills. We were arguing daily.

Life was testing both of us. Once in awhile I landed some work and took full advantage of the opportunities. But, sometimes ones breaking point is just that. Some days were just absolutely horrible between us and we started with counselling. I was really messed up by the whole chain of events from the last several months of our relationship and we were actually not meant for each other after all, although I never wanted to believe that. By August 1996, Hayden's first birthday, After several weeks of verbal fights and miscommunication I was subpoenaed at work. Jo quickly ended our relationship.

It was devastating to say the least. I never saw it coming. I was having a super shitty time at this point and I couldn't handle much of anything. I never even thought of us separate from our children.

But, with a restraining order and her friends and family by her side (and me all alone), I was forced to leave. We were married for fifteen months and our son had just turned one. I had to walk away, forcibly I might add. I wanted to fix things, I wanted her to love me. I felt I let Dusty and Hayden down and would never be the father I had hoped to be.

Instead I found myself constantly searching for answers but finding the bottle instead. Beers, joints—whatever it took to get through the days and nights of absolute depression and a broken heart. I found a place to live, a mice-ridden cabin off the edge of town. I lost my job and found myself with no future anymore. I wanted to kill myself daily, for weeks on end. But, one thing kept stopping me. Jo was never going to bring me down. I was stronger than I ever thought I could be.

One night something clicked in my hot head of confusion and misery. I needed closure. I needed to know who I was. What am I? Where am I supposed to go? Why am I this way? So many questions entered my brain and I needed answers, closure and a new heading. Certain thoughts dictated my life and I wanted to know why.

I decided I had to find my father.

I looked up to my two older step brothers for guidance, love and support, and I just had no one else to lean on. The oldest, Milan, moved back to Ontario to pursue his cabinet making business when I was around twelve. So, it was difficult to connect with him and when I did it was usually when I was going through some hardship. I think he always thought of me as a broken kid that needed discipline and to be put in my place. Whenever I had the opportunity to visit him I always tried to pay him the utmost respect. But, his rough attitude towards me broke me down more than I was willing to take. So, our relationship never gave me the hope and direction I was looking for. But, he knew of my father and where he might be. Before my 30th birthday I flew back east to ask my brother to help me.

We drove in the afternoon of a November day, it was dark and stormy along the way.

"I think this is it, his restaurant," said Milan.

The sign out front of the single story brick and mortar building way outside the town of Peterborough read: "Denbar's Steak Chalet."

"Is it really? Guess it makes sense. Den is short for Dennis, my father's name is Zdenek, which means Dennis in English. It's also my middle name," I said to Milan while I unsnapped my seatbelt.

"And bars is short for Bartak I guess, Henry," Milan replied. "I will stay here for you, OK?"

I nodded and left his van, walking up the few stairs to the front door. As I stepped inside I noticed the floor was made of rounds of wood that were set in a glossy finish. The character of the inside was European: old country pictures, statuettes, plates and beer steins on the walls and shelves all around. There were old and young couples sitting at round tables with candles lit on top. The busboy was dressed in a loose suit and tie, the waitresses wore a Scandinavian theme.

"Hello, may I help you?" one waitress asked me.

"Yes, I'd like to sit down for dinner," I replied.

I most definitely did not look the part for eating there. My stormrider jean jacket, a pair of ripped old jeans, and sneakers on. And, I was alone.

"How is this?" The waitress took me to a table at the side of the room.

"Sure, you bet. Looks good!" I replied, taking my seat. "I would love a double Jack and Coke please," I said.

She handed me the menu and removed the second setting from the table.

"I will be back with your drink, and to take your order OK?" she said.

I swallowed my drink and thought, *What the fuck am I doing? What if he is not here? What if he is? Look at the couples here, they all seem so happy and in love. I am here and scared, nervous and this first drink just hit me.* "Excuse me, may I have another drink please?" I asked the busboy as he walked past.

"I will let your waitress know, sir," he replied.

Whatever happened I figured I made it this far. I didn't feel any resentment or anger. I just needed to meet the guy who is my father. But first I'd better eat.

After several drinks, a big ass steak, escargot, sherbet to cleanse my palate, and crème brûlée for desert, the bill arrived.

"Ummm, I don't think I will pay this," I told the Scandinavian-dressed waitress.

Her eyes popped out and she was not sure what I just said. "Is there a problem with the bill or your meal?" she asked me.

I looked at her, my eyes blurred by the drinks, and went for it! "Yes, I'd like to see the owner, please," I said.

My heart was pounding and sweat beaded on my forehead as she retreated to the kitchen. A quick minute later, a tall, older gentleman dressed in chef's attire approached the table. I remained in my seat, not sure what was happening. The drinks seemed to hit all at once.

"Is there a problem with the bill? You ask for me?" the chef said, standing at the edge of the table.

"Yes, there is," I replied. I looked straight into his eyes and said, "I am your son."

The man looked into my eyes, staring for a moment. "I always knew you would come and find me," he said as his hands fell onto the table. "My legs are giving out, I will sit down for a moment OK?"

I just nodded. As he sat down, I broke down in tears, with years of pent up memories and emotions leaking uncontrollably down my face. He leaned over and we hugged for the first time. All of a sudden I felt different, new, whole, confident again.

"Will you stay here for the night and we can talk more after I close the restaurant later?" he asked

"That's a good idea," I said.

The following day I met my father and his wife for lunch and found out I have a younger sister! Her name is Carmen. She is half east Indian and half Czech. She is beautiful, tall, slender, and has long black hair with fine facial features. When we met, she showed me the only picture she held onto for years in her purse. It was me when I was just a kid, and it was all she knew of me. She always wondered where or who I was, and when we finally met we hit it off. We bonded immediately! I was not the young runt anymore, I had someone that needed me and it gave me the spark to keep going.

We spent a few days together in Peterborough. After that, I left for Vancouver to visit my mother who had recently been released from the hospital. She was doing a lot better and was starting over with an apartment in the east end. Keeping in touch with my mother was something we both needed. She told me how she felt guilty about my childhood and how she wished to make things better. In my older years, I discovered the love a parent has for their children. It was always an absolute pleasure to see my mother with a smile. I confided in her and sought advice when I visited her. We spoke openly and she knew just the right things to say to me. She told me I needed a change, a chance to be happy again. We spoke of our time together in Australia and how much I regretted being a snot-nosed kid to her when we were there. It was not nice of me to cheat her of the time with her brother. I wanted to make things right, for her, for me.

Back in Campbell River a few weeks later I tried so hard to make things right with Jo and our family. But, there was nothing to mend. It was over, my heart was sunk and my life with my son turned out to be the most devastating and heartbreaking part of my life. I was so close to him yet so far away. I decided that far away may be what was meant for me. I made plans with my cousins, Michelle and Magda in Australia, that I was coming for a visit. But, first I needed to clean myself up some.

I was on the way to the liquor store to drown my sorrow when something clicked. I drove past the store and ended up at the local gym. I signed up and decided that nothing was ever going to knock me down again. I was a tough guy, but mentally I was weak. The next ten months I dive into eating right, studying the foods, proteins, carbs, fats, building muscles and thinking positive. Seven days a week, sometimes twice or three times a day, I would be training. Running, diets, fitness contests, strong man competitions, my new friends were all in the gym. Life seemed to be more controlled, more fulfilling. I would see Hayden when I was allowed to and I gave him all my attention. I wanted him all to myself, to love and care for him. I was on a mission now to better myself, for him. That is my goal.

Chapter 9 – Australia and Beyond

"I'd like 'Hayden' tattooed on my arm, please. He is my son and I figure if I can't have him then at least he can still come with me," I told the fella who is going to ink my boy's name on my right arm.

"Where you going?" said this tall, tattoo-sleeved young guy. He's wearing a red t-shirt and blue jeans that are being held up with purple suspenders. The suspenders have marijuana leaves printed on them.

"Australia!" I replied with a huge smile. I felt great, I was in the best shape of my life even though I was only twenty nine years old. "I have family there and I am going for a while, not sure if I am coming back," I said. Looking around at the walls of pictures in his parlour I saw a Canadian flag. "I'd like this under my son's name as well, OK? And write: 'Born in Canada' around the flag."

As I went through security at the Vancouver airport three weeks later, I was pulled aside. "Sir, would you please come with me?" a tall, well dressed, clean cut man wearing glasses said to me. He was in his thirties, I figure, and was motioning me to leave the line up.

"Huh? Yeah sure, I guess. Where we going?" I asked him.

"Are you military?" he asked me as I followed him. I noticed two more security men behind me.

"Huh? No. Why?" I replied.

"Your tattoo, is that airborne?" he said, pointing at my arm.

"Oh, no, it is a Harley sign actually," I said back. I guess with my buzz cut, muscle shirt, and my physical fitness, I could see how he would think that. I followed him with the security behind into a closed room.

"Tell me, sir, have you ever been arrested or charged with a crime?" the security man asked me. "You want to tell me the truth because we can look you up. I'm giving you the opportunity to be honest with me," he said.

I told him that I had a pardon from some past mistakes but I am a changed man now.

"Really? And for what?" he asked.

After 40 minutes of drilling me and checking my history on the computers, the three of them talked in another room, looking at me through the glass in the doors. Then one of them came out to the counter and I stood up. I knew my flight was delayed and I was nervous as fuck that I was not going to make it.

"Well Henry, my supervisor figures that since you are not staying in the United States and just stopping for a change of flight, and that you have been honest about your past, he flipped a coin. And you won. It's your lucky day pal, you best hurry cause everyone on the plane is waiting for you," he said as he handed me my passport.

I grabbed it and my backpack and tumbled out of the security room. I madly ran straight for the plane that had been delayed over thirty minutes because of me! As I walked through the aisles to my seat, all I saw were eyes from dozens of passengers on me. Wiping the sweat off my forehead with my shirt I leaned back in my chair and put my seatbelt on. As the plane rolled down the runway I looked to the left to see who my neighbour was. A cute, innocent looking younger woman with brown eyes and brown shoulder-length hair with a beaded little purse-type pouch hanging off her neck was sitting there.

"Hi, how you doing?" I asked. The plane was just leaving the tarmac and was shaky throughout the interior. She held the arm rests tightly. "Nervous? It's OK, we are alright. Look, we are up," I said.

The cabin of the airliner was quiet except the loud sounds of metal on metal, wind thrusting on the outer shell of this beast with wings. Up, up almost completely vertical the forces pulled us back into the seat. The plane was full and for the moment, everyone deep down were having the same thoughts: "I hope I don't die in a plane crash."

This adorable little Mexican girl sitting next to me couldn't understand a word I was saying to her. And I hadn't a clue what she is talking about either. But, I could tell by her facial expressions that she didn't scare easily and was quite relaxed. The plane started to level off and murmurs escalated into full out conversations. The seatbelt sign turned off and people began moving around. Soon the loud noises from outside were a lot quieter.

"Where, w-h-e-r-e a-r-e y-o-u g-o-i-n-g?" I said quite slowly with deliberate pronouncements of each letter with my hands and arms flailing about. I sketched a plane in the sky going away. She watched me and tried to figure out what the hell that I was trying to say.

"India, I go to India," she said. For the next ten hours we had conversation after conversation, each time understanding one another more and more. This was just another experience and it would not be my last. I bought a bottle of Bailey's from the Duty Free shop prior to being interrogated by the airport authority. Legna and I would finished that bottle and just had a super time getting to know one another. We would fall asleep, wake up a couple hours later, talk and continue with the hand sketches in the air in order to fully convey our meanings.

There was an eighteen-hour layover in Kuala Lumpur, Malaysia, and we arrived about nine o'clock in the evening. Our luggage was being transferred and a handful of passengers had to stay longer and we received hotel rooms. Legna was the very last person in line and by her turn at the reception, all the rooms were gone.

"It's OK Legna, there are always two beds in a room. You can stay with me!" I told her and the little Asian lady in a suit and bow tie at reception. This was a nice hotel for sure and I was excited about some company, especially hers. "C'mon, I wont bite! We will have fun. Maybe we can see some of the city tomorrow?" I told her.

She looked up at me and smiled, nodding her head. I grabbed one of her bags and my room key, and headed straight to the bar!

After getting settled in our room, Legna was at ease, especially having known me for the twelve or so hours. I was no threat at all. And it's how I tend to be, a gentleman always. I was not that rough, tough doorman at the rail anymore. Let's just enjoy every moment and go with it. I bought eight bottles of beer from the bar just as they closed. They were warm because the air was humid and stifling, so we got a bucket with ice.

"There is a pool on the roof, Legna, let's go and enjoy the night for a while," I said, grabbing the bucket of beers and a towel. We headed up the elevator to the roof.

The next day, we set out to see downtown Kuala Lumpur. There was a full day to kill before her plane left for India. Mine was soon after hers to Sydney, Australia. By now, our communication skills required less arm movement and it was more that we just understood each other. We spent the next several hours exploring this new city and the different people in a different culture. We tried different food and drinks and enriched our minds with the differences in our own countries. By the afternoon we made it back to the hotel room and gathered our belongings.

"This has been really great getting to know you, Legna. I really hope you are safe travelling through India by yourself. And let's keep in touch, OK? There is this new website on the internet called Facebook. We can keep in touch, okay?" I said as I wrapped my arms around this little adorable Mexican girl.

And just like that, she was gone. I felt alone. It was quiet and the short hour I had to kill before boarding my flight was enjoyable. I had made a friend, we had a wonderful time together travelling thousands of miles to a different culture and country. I felt like this was a warm-up, a lesson on how to deal with the moments. There were going to be a lot of these moments, especially starting with my next flight. Legna and I kept in touch over Facebook for eighteen years till we met again. This time I would finally visit Mexico and see my little adorable Mexican girl again.

December 15, 1999, it was around 3-ish in the afternoon.

"Welcome to Sydney, Australia!" came the steward's voice over the loudspeaker on the place. "The local mean temperature is 38 degrees Celsius but with 90 percent humidity the real feel is about 44. So, enjoy and be safe travelling through or just hitting the beaches!"

It was different, smelled different, felt strange but euphoric throughout my senses. The smell of the humidity and the mixture of hot asphalt, hot rubber from the wheels of the plane, to sweat now dripping off everyone as the cabin doors opened. The warm air flowed throughout. I grabbed my backpack from the overhead compartment, and elbows came from all directions as others were scrambling to get their shit and leave the oven of a plane. I stepped out onto the gangway and I was hit by an invisible wall of fire. The heat was instantly unbearable to the senses. But, I was there. Everything in front of me was what I made of it, and this was going to be fantastic!!

I was excited to see Michelle, Magda and my Aunt Jana again. I jumped on the bus to the city. A few hours and several asks for directions later, I found the address I was looking for. Michelle was expecting me but I wasn't able to touch base with her during my trip. I pressed the buzzer and waited. I had my backpack on, and held a duffel bag in one hand and a Foster's beer in the other. I had gone into a store while on route to my destination.

"Hello?" comes through the speaker.

"It's Henry from Canada here," I said.

"HENRY!! C'mon in!"

It was great to see Michelle. She was gorgeous, had long, blonde, straight hair with bangs over her marble-blue eyes. In the first two days, I found out she was a neat freak. She seemed to always have something that needed to be done yesterday. It was great getting to know my cousin, even though it seemed Magda was not interested in meeting me again. Michelle and I related I think a bit more because we are the same age and for the most part we kept in touch. Unfortunately, Michelle was so super busy with work and her personal life that she didn't have the spare time for me. I visited Sydney, Bondi Beach and Kings Cross with everything in between on my own, but I didn't let that stop me from enjoying myself. But, over the next four or five days I didn't feel so comfortable with my cousin. She obviously was going through her own path in life and I decided I be better off to continue my adventure.

On my sixth day in Australia I jumped on a bus up the coast. There were people from all over the world on the bus. Same people as me, with similar stories to tell.

"Hi! Where are you from?" I asked the blonde sitting next to me. I was just on top, I felt so awesome! Conversations were endless and beautiful women bountiful. I landed in Port Macquarie, a small town on the east coast, about five or six hours north of Sydney. Lindels Hostel was just on the edge of town. It was a two story home with a huge front porch that had a sloped, shingled roof over it. Along the deck of the front porch, which was the entire size of the home, were couches, chairs and tables with ashtrays and beer bottles on them. Stairs leading me up to the front porch were newly painted and still a bit tacky.

"Hallo mate, my name is Paul. I work here and can help you, are you wanting a bed?" said a balding, round-headed thin man wearing John Lennon-style glasses. He reached out to help me with my bag. He had white paint droppings all over him and especially his hands. A beer in one, and a smoke in the other I let him take my bag and followed him inside.

"This here is the common area and kitchen. How long you staying?" Paul asked me as he greeted other people in the rooms we passed. Some looked like they were just getting up or on their way to bed.

"Ummm, I am not sure really. No particular place to go and in no rush. How about a few days to start?" I replied.

He looked over at me with a smile that showed off his two missing teeth. He said I should stick around for the Christmas week festivities. The owners of the hostel were having a Christmas party and some of the others had extended their stay.

"Well, this is where you can stay. There are eight per room so we have rules and regulations for respect of the others. This pamphlet outlines the House Rules. Now get settled and join us on the porch. I will introduce you to the others."

Instantly I felt at ease with Paul the Aussie, as I called him. He told me what to check every day and hooked me up with other tour operators in the town. I was going for wine tours, rainforest, waterfalls tours and meeting people from all over. I was in the best shape as well, so it was the best time in my life to experience all this. Unbelievable! I went from not having a drop of alcohol for three months to drinking every day. And having so much fun—long overdue.

And just like that it was Christmas! Three guys from the United Kingdom came to the hostel. Dave was in his late twenties and losing his hair already. He had a strong English accent, which was hard to understand when he spoke fast. Mark was the same age, an athletic type. He was an innocent, good looking guy with reddish blonde hair. And finally, Peter was shorter than the other two, bigger belly, with curly brown hair and glasses. We sat on the porch drinking with Paul the Aussie and the new tourists coming in. Some of the Sheilas "were outstanding talent" as Paul would say.

"Merry Christmas to you darling," he said as he flipped his cowboy hat off at them coming up the stairs. Then there was the three drunken Englishmen greeting: "Halo, thar Sheila, Santa's inside," all said in broken harmony. Then they would break out laughing and I was right there with them.

The second week into staying at Lindel's, the owner had an offer for me. "Henry, are you enjoying yourself? Do you like our town?"

"Of course," I said.

"I just had someone leave today, I can use a new helper if you'd like to stay here for a while?" he offered.

That had my attention for sure and I agreed to stick around. I would change linen on the beds and keep the floors clean in exchange for a free room. I also started selling fruit at a corner stand for a local guy, which gave me some extra cash. The three English guys and I hung out each night at the local night clubs and the beaches after. You see, there were only three places to go in this small beach town but they were open from eleven at night till six in the morning. Every person going through town even for a night would be steered to one of these clubs. Being Canadian alone introduced me to many people and new experiences. We were having the time of our lives!

Mark, Dave and Peter were enjoying themselves so much they decided to stay through the New Years and then some. I was working for the hostel, and steering new customers to local tours and bringing my mates the perks of new introductions.

We kayaked with the dolphins, took forest and wine tours, and just met new people daily. We were even invited to locals' places for barbecues and parties. Tammy invited us to her place in the town of Tamworth, a few hundred kilometres inland and home of the biggest cowboy boot in the world. Peter decided he didn't want to go and we tried our best to talk him into it, but he'd have none of it. So, we rented a car and hit the road to party with some Aussie women.

"OK mate, if we don't make it back by Monday then call the authorities," I said to Peter.

Our older model falcon four door wasn't pretty, but it was cheap to rent. Mark followed the map Paul gave us, and I sat in the back as Dave drove. It took us a couple of hours driving inland to get far from the coast and deep into the mountains. The drive itself was more enjoyable because we had reefer and beers. Just enjoying the ride.

"Dave pull over at that petro station, we have not one till now. Who knows what's after this. According to the map we are only halfway to Tamworth," Mark yelled over the radio.

"OK! OK!" he yelled back, pulling up to one of the older style gas pumps you wouldn't see anymore back home. Just out in the middle of nowhere stood this small 70s-style gas station with two pumps. The car ahead sped away, dust kicking up as we stopped in the cloud next to the pump. Mark jumped out and started pumping the petrol. Dave and Mark tried tofigure out the map and decided we were headed in the right direction. I sat in the back, rolling a joint for our next leg of the journey.

"Hey, where y'all from? Here, I can do that. I work here and I can finish pumping your petrol," said an Aussie guy with a cowboy hat and boots, wearing jeans and a t-shirt. He took the nozzle from Mark.

"Sure, you bet, sir," said Mark. He thinks to himself, this cowboy doesn't look any older than we are.

"So, where you all headed?" he asked.

"Tamworth to party," said Dave. "Are we headed the right way?"

"Yeah sure. Another three hundred kilometers that way you reach Tamworth. You all have some Sheilas there do you? I tell you what, I am having a party too! My place is closer, I have waterfalls and Sheilas there. I will call my mate and start the barby," he said.

This sounded like a great alternative to driving all the way to Tamworth. Dave looked relieved now that he was assured of the direction, and Mark was into the closeness of a good time.

"Thirty-five even mates, I am actually just finishing my shift here. I will go inside and pay your petrol and tell them I am leaving. Then just follow me to my place, I will call my mate and give him the heads-up," said the cowboy as Dave handed him the money.

Dave got back into the driver's seat, Mark had the map out and I was watching Aussie cowboy walk to the front door of the gas station. But, instead of grabbing the door and going inside, he cut left and went behind the station.

"Hey guys! Guess what?" and just as I am about to tell them, a huge pick-up truck pulled in front of us. The cowboy was driving and waving his hat for us to follow. Dave changed gear and hit the gas. We were right on cowboy's heels with dust clouds behind us.

"What's up HENRY? You said something?" Mark yelled.

"Yeah! I was going to tell you guys that we just ripped off the station!" I yelled.

"What? Are you serious? How can that be? Cowboy works there," Mark said over the music.

"Because he obviously does not work there!" I replied. I told them what I saw while we still followed him through the forest. Minutes went by and I was trying to convince Mark and Dave that cowboy was not who he appeared to be. Meanwhile, cowboy was driving erratically and kept kicking dust off the gravel shoulder at us. My gut feeling was we were being led astray and I didn't want any part of it.

"Stop! Let me out! You two can go but I want you to let me out. Honestly, I don't feel right with this guy," I said. All of a sudden we seemed to drive out of the forest and mountain range and now were into clear open flats for a long ways.

There is still nothing in sight: no homes, farms or civilization but one side road off to the right.

"Listen, if he takes this road I want you to stop! Let me out. I am telling you guys!!" I yelled from the back seat.

Just then, the pick-up turned and dust kicked up off the gravel road.

"Where's the waterfalls? Huh? It's all flat here. Where's the hill with water? Stop please! Let me out now!" I was grabbing the guys' shoulders to get my point across. Dave slammed on the brakes and I was thrust forward.

"We will stop, but we're in this together. We'll just tell him we changed our minds," said Dave.

We pulled off to the edge of the gravel road just as cowboy and his pick-up turned right onto the side road.

"Look, at him! He looks pissed" I said. We lost him for a second while the dust cloud enveloped him. His arms were in the air and he was yelling at us; it's obvious that his fun-like demeanour was over.

"What are you doing?? Why did you stop? We are almost there!!" he yelled.

Mark and Dave looked at each other, and it was like everything I had been trying to tell them finally snapped together. Dave shoved the car into gear, hit the gas and we sped off kicking gravel up and spraying cowboy and his pickup. Cowboy threw his hat to the ground and kicked his truck, screaming profanities in a cloud of dust.

For the first few minutes we were silent, then Mark said, "Where were the waterfalls if there was no mountain?" We couldn't believe what just happened or even more what might have happened to us if we were so naïve as to continue following him. We headed for Tamworth as wiser travelers. About three years later I watched a movie called *Wolf Creek* and it is about a serial killer in Australia. To this day I wonder just how close we came to some monstrous demise. The killer in the movie skinned his victims while they hung on meat hooks in a barn. He was caught only after one victim escaped.

When we got back, Mark and Dave hooked back up with their third musketeer and they continued their holiday through Australia. I stayed on at the hostel and started a part time job as a doorman at one of the night clubs. I was the only Canadian doorman in town and I fit right in. The local girls were definitely interested in meeting me, the Canadian! Every weekend I worked for some cash at the Down Under Night Club. The establishment was actually downstairs in a larger building. The staff were very friendly people and the management, I think, was a bit of a joke to them. "Big Tim" was the manager, an older Aussie guy who weighed around four hundred pounds and made bets to see who could smash the Canadian. The bets were on when the biggest pair of men walked in late one Saturday afternoon. They were two couples of aboriginal decent—Samoans, maybe. The largest breed of human on earth, they were obviously a father and son with their female partners. It was a quiet day with only a few patrons in the Down Under.

"Hey Canadian boy, c'mon here let's have a word," Tim said from behind the bar. I was standing at the bottom of the stairs and welcomed the new patrons inside. I looked at this huge tub of a guy talking to a couple of his other doorman and the waiter. They exchanged money and laughed so loud it echoed in the bar.

I walked over, "Yes Tim, what's up?"

He scratched his balding head and a few strands popped out and lodged between his fingers. He looked over at his waitress who was bringing a tray of beverages to the father and son party of four.

"I want you to go over and get those out of here, they are not welcomed here," he said loud enough for everyone to hear.

I looked over at the table and four of them were pretending not to have heard anything.

"They have not done anything," I said to the God 'o Mighty here.

"We don't serve Abby's here, get them out before they start something." He motioned the other doorman to help me.

"No, I can do this by myself. And we won't have any problems, OK?"

I walked over to the table. Beavis and Butthead were at the bar anticipating me to get into fisticuffs with the father and son but I'd been doing this awhile and I was smart about dealing with situations. After chatting for a couple of minutes, I looked over at Tim and his crony just to reassure them I had the situation handled. And few minutes more went by, the four nice people finished their drinks, stood up, shook my hand and left. They were going up the stairs as I walked back to Beavis and Butthead, winked and said, "Not a problem boss, I got them out."

Back at Lindel's Hostel I started a barbecue dinner special every night. The owner helped me get started with his 16x30 flat grill barbecue out back next to the outdoor swimming pool. I spent most afternoons there meeting the new tourists. Coming from all over the world, they loved to be fed by the handsome Canadian! I received a lot of compliments and I loved every minute of it. The outdoor tables were full of a dozen or more every night for dinner. Five bucks a plate for a meal and I always sold out. With a swim right after, there were four days in three months that I did not drink!

I went to a Champion's Gym across the street every morning. It was a professional bodybuilder's place. I was taught a few things training with these guys. By lunch I was headed to the local beaches, or hooking up tours with my local friends and the new tourists. I didn't mind staying in one town for three months, my whole time in Australia. I met some great people, learned more of the culture and local foods. But, soon my time was coming to an end unless I ignored my visa and decided to stay. And I seriously thought about it. But, I was tapped of funds. I earned what I could and enjoyed every day. My birthday was a couple of days away and I would leave for Sydney the next morning. I would spend a week hanging out in Sydney before flying back.

"Well, your last day here, Henry. I will miss you, Mate, it's been really nice having you here," Paul lifted his beer to give me a cheers. A cigarette hanging from his mouth, he smiled and patted me on the shoulder. I raised my beer and *clang* went the bottles. The owners, Wil and Di, organized a dinner and cake while Paul organized every person who came through the front door on the porch for a birthday/going away party for Henry the Canadian!! By two in the afternoon Paul was smashed and took a nap, while I decided to join the other tourists at the pool. The sun shone so much and the heat was unbearable at times, but I loved it. I was grabbing every minute I could to the fullest. I was dark tanned and feeling awesome from the gym every day.

Paul woke up and we carried on drinking on the front porch with a few others that were staying there when we all noticed a motorbike pull up. She was a gorgeous young woman with a cut crew cut. She climbed the stairs and we saw her leather jacket was unzipped halfway to reveal her tank top underneath. She was sweating and we could see the clear glistening trail that ran from her head down her throat and between her breasts. She wore a proper leather outfit with pants and boots. She looked HOT; a gorgeous babe on a bike.

"Hello, my name is Letitia. I would like a room please," she said, looking at me with her green eyes. I was a mess inside.

"Paul, get her a room, eh?" I nudged him with my elbow. "Paul here will set you up OK, then when you are settled please join us for my birthday party tonight!" Standing beside Paul, I opened the door for her.

I bet it wasn't fifteen minutes before Letitia was back and sitting right next to me. Over the next several hours and into the evening everyone was very drunk and having the most fun and laughs. One by one people went to bed to pass out, a couple decided to sleep right where they were on the front porch. The night was clammy, hot and muggy. The stars were so extra bright, we saw the odd shooting star. Listening to the local music station, Letitia and I were the last survivors and we decided a midnight swim was in order. I will never forget that midnight swim under the stars with a beautiful young Aussie babe who had just started her bike ride around Australia. I was the first night of her adventure. We had so much fun together and we felt so good touching one another that the next day when I had to leave for Sydney, she came with me even though that's where she'd come from the day before!

She eventually put her adventure driving on hold for the week. We rented a private room in a hostel and spent every minute together for most of the next week (mostly in the room). This was the last week I was in Australia and the most memorable experience for both of us. She went with me to the airport and waved me off. I would think that her adventure was just as memorable but she was just starting her year-long sabbatical. We kept in touch for a few years, hoping I would make it back. But, I had the responsibility of my son to acknowledge and Letitia found herself a husband. To this day I have never had such an intense romance in a short moment like that.

I was looking forward to seeing my son again. I felt reborn, I knew great positive opportunities were at hand for me. I had no place called home, but that didn't bother me. I had no job, no car but that didn't bother me. I had a feeling of greatness and inspiration that overwhelmed all else. I would not worry about what I could not control and concentrated on putting one foot in front of the other.

The first person I visited when I got back was my mother. I had to make sure she was OK and I slept on her couch for a couple of nights. She always appreciated any visits from her boys and an opportunity to feed us. My favourite meal is from her old country: Czech dumplings with cabbage and pork. She taught me how to make it her way. We enjoyed our visit then I made my way back to the Island. The next person I wanted to see was my son.

Chapter 10 – What Can Happen Now?

2000-2005

There was a knock at the door, I knew who it was. I had been watching the clock and listening for someone to drive up the gravel driveway. Not long after, I heard the crunching sounds of gravel. I wanted to show her how much I regretted everything that happened between us and all I wanted was my family back. I felt replenished from my holidays and I had high hopes of a new beginning, but lessons taught me to take things at face value sometimes and my ex-wife had made it very clear on several occasions that there was no future between us.

"What is done is done, Henry. It's never the same," she told me the last time I attempted to make amends.

My whole life I was denied my childhood and now my son's childhood? I was destroying myself in search of a very much desired yet vacant feeling: to be loved. *Why me? Why am I punished like this?* I constantly asked myself, especially when I drank. I got drunk on a regular basis to cloud the negative feelings that brewed whenever I missed Hayden. I never wanted to be alone growing up. As a child, I waited for someone to come home after school and as a young man I only experienced a family for a very short time. I knew I had made huge mistakes that cost me everything that was important, and the worst part were the consequences. Like never seeing my son ever again and losing the opportunity to feel loved. I hope my son never feels the same.

I needed the getaway. I felt kind of secure and somewhat grounded again. I could handle any situation with more positive control now. As I reached for the door handle my hands were sweaty and my mouth was dry but I was excited beyond the stars to see my son. *What shall I teach him this time?* I wondered, cause my times were seldom and I needed to take advantage of every opportunity to teach my son things I knew. *Pass on my fatherly wisdom*, I thought. I wanted to teach my boy everything and I wanted him to be proud of me and of himself one day. I wanted him to be grateful for having a father who wants to be in his life.

I opened the door and the boys were standing on either side of their gorgeous mother. Hayden has my nose, jawline, blue eyes and big shoulders, but he definitely has her looks and her height. He was smiling and obviously excited, and I had goosebumps. He jumped into my arms and I held him tight. I opened my eyes to look at Jo; she was as beautiful as when we first met.

"Oh! Hi, well, here we are. Say hello to your father, Hayden," she said with hesitation.

"Hi Dad!"

I held out my arms for Dustin, "Hi Dust, how are you doing?"

He jumped in as well and I held them both tightly. I let them loose to go inside and check out their new home.

"Well, this all works out. I am actually going to Victoria for the weekend and you are on the way, mind if I come inside?" she walked in and looked around.

I grabbed the boys' luggage to bring inside. Hayden found my Xbox and sat down in front on the rug, turning on the television. I turned around from the door about to set the luggage aside when she stepped up close to me and quietly said, "You are living well, very nice furnishings you have. You take care of yourself while we are getting by?"

The smell of her hair jumps to my nose, reminding me of a time long ago. She abruptly walked through my place and her smile turned inside out. I stepped aside to let her pass and she started questioning me. I told her I wanted to have a nice place for my kids. But, being a narcissist she is never wrong. A big part of our disagreements came from her thought that our relationship destruction was 100% my fault. There was always another reason that triggered her actions, never owning her mistakes but blaming others. The kids had always been a weapon for her, gradually growing a gap between us so large eventually everyone is against me.

She told Hayden and Dustin to grab their stuff.

"But Mom! I just got here, and am in the middle of a game," Hayden yelled, glued to the tube.

She grabbed his arm and apologized for what their father was making her do. And she promptly took the boys and left as quickly as she came in. I didn't understand what just happened. I was trying to make things better between us and she was not communicating with me. Instead of seeking a healthier relationship, all efforts were in vain. How could I do the right things if I didn't know what was expected from me? No one ever taught me these things in life. I was frustrated and felt I had failed my boys.

This "waiting" for the time I could spend with Hayden became normal over the next several years. Everyone always told me, "Henry, just wait till he is older, he will come around."

I wouldn't have any communication with my ex-wife because situations became more volatile and ended poorly for everyone. I sometimes opened lines with her but as soon as our conversations turned sideways I stopped all together. I started only communicating with my son and I worked constantly on holding and building a relationship with him. He was still with his mother in Campbell river and I would not miss my weekends to be with him. I would work in Langford or Victoria all week, but when my weekend came I drove the 3 to 4 hours it took to get there. I never missed a weekend in three years, even rented a second place for me and Hayden to call home in Campbell River. We had our traditional breakfast at Banners Restaurant, followed by a matinee at the local movie theatre. The cameraman was so used to seeing us, he gave Hayden and I tours of the theatre and free popcorn. We did this every weekend we had together.

Hayden was probably about eight years old at this time. It was always too bad his mother and I couldn't be more sympathetic to each other but I didn't let her come between my son and I, or Dustin. It seemed to give their mother ammunition for her weapons, constantly putting the boys in the middle. I don't want to make myself an innocent person here; every relationship exists around two people and their differences. This time, now looking back at the three years that I was able to see Hayden every second weekend. I never missed my weekend, I drove up island and made a second home for us there. We had our routine, breakfast at Banners Restaurant followed by an afternoon movie. Then we'd walk on the pier and do a little fishing. I feel fortunate that I had the opportunity to bond with my son.

All within a few months of this short time frame, my ex-wife decided to take me to court, again attempting to get what money she felt she deserved. Work on the island is very seasonal and I was working for a new company out of Nanaimo. So, quickly it seemed I was back fighting depression again, always triggered by the constant negativity from my ex-wife, lawyers, family maintenance, and always fighting with doing the right thing when I just wanted everything to be OK. And I wanted my son; I needed him just as he needed me.

My mother needed me as well. I got a call from Tomas in Prince George where he was bringing up his family.

"Hey bro, how are you? Hey, Mom needs you to go see her. OK? I would but I have an important meeting this week plus you're closer. Sounds like she stopped taking her medication again. Can you go?"

I was on the ferry the next morning, hoping I wouldn't lose my job. There was a good chance I would because I had just started and didn't know how long I would be on the mainland. I hated having to deal with the hospitals and committing my mother every time there was an episode. But, without me or Tomas she was in a really bad place.

The worst was lying to her of my intentions: "No mom, seriously, I am just taking us out for lunch. I just want to see you and make sure you are alright," I told her, knowing the hospital was expecting us because I called them before we left her place. "I am here because I love you, Mommy. I can help you as much as I can."

Once the doctors treated her, her anxieties were lower and she was calmer. Granted, it all came from the several medications that she took and it was no wonder she fought to get off them all. Sometimes I had to miss my visits with Hayden because I was in East Vancouver taking care of my mother. I sometimes spent a couple or few weeks getting my mother's affairs in order while thinking of what I had planned to do with my son. I never felt good about myself when mom was ill. She was the only person I knew who loved me regardless of who I was or what I did, and I would be there for her as much as I could. I always thought it would all work in the end.

I did lose my job after starting just a month prior but I believe life steers an individual in the direction one needs to go. So far, I had gone through several employers over the few years due to various reasons ranging from shortage of work, not enough experience, or I didn't fit in and just quit. Tried to go with the flow but sometimes life just throws it all at you at once just to test you.

Depression had been a cloud for me for years. I really wanted to feel better, do better, be a better father, a better man. I was failing and my trip to Australia was a memory. I was looking for a new employer, bills were falling behind and I found myself constantly struggling on my own. I was dealing with my life but I didn't have anyone to share my weaknesses, scares, tears, smiles and decisions with. If I did feel comfortable talking to someone it seemed to backfire on me. I always had a "look," you know? It was a big, intimidating, mean look about me that most people took the wrong way. Did I ever make the correct decisions? Because I always seemed to be in repair mode.

I still worked part time at the bar for the extra cash. Hard earned paychecks some nights, putting my life on the line for patrons I didn't even know. Defending them against bad people, gangs, crack heads, ex-cons, bikers, stoners you name it. One night I recall working for a club that was at the Howard Johnson Hotel in Nanaimo. The Grizzly Bar, a drinking establishment with pool tables and DJ booth with a dance floor was upstairs. Underneath was the Basement Nightclub. That's the name!

This was a very busy night, we had hip hop artists and it was the last week of the month—welfare week. Super busy because everyone was rich for a few days. I had three hired doormen at the front doors, a few more floating through the establishment. I was dealing with a situation by the smoking area off to the side of the bar when I heard someone calling over the loudspeakers.

"We need a doorman on the dance floor now!" and the announcement was quickly repeated.

I pushed my way through the crowded rooms of people to find a young black guy lying on the floor with his arms protecting the back of his head. There were 7-10 short Asian dudes breaking their full beer bottles on the guy's head. There was blood everywhere and I reached down to grab the guy, shielding him from the hits with my other arm. I wrap my arm under his and we quickly made our way through the crowd to a panic room we had just for such an occasion. This whole time a few other situations erupted that kept the other security guys occupied.

"C'mon buddy get inside and lock the door, I got this" I yelled at the black dude who was bleeding everywhere from the cuts on his head.

Two others joined him inside the room and they locked the door. I turned around to face the Asians with bottles and knives in their hands. They were screaming at me in two languages but I stood guard.

"There is no way I can let you through so get out of here, now!" I yelled at them repeatedly.

We had a standoff in the narrow hallway for several minutes, when in the distance I heard the police entering through the front doors. Luckily, I didn't have to escalate the situation more and the group of Asians quickly dispersed past the dance floor and into the crowd. A couple of weeks later I found out the black dude received over 70 stitches throughout his face and head. And the guy was claiming the doormen didn't do their job correctly. I said he be dead if I didn't. Guess he messed around with the wrong people.

When I am not working in the bar, or on a construction site, or even on stage or in front of the camera, I enjoy exercise and keeping myself motivated by the challenges of weight lifting, swimming, and sports. I have always been active and really enjoy the outdoors, and activities such as hiking, camping, fishing give me a freedom to explore true inner peace. Operating excavators seems to be more emotionally draining just because of the "dog eat dog" atmosphere, so I applied and was accepted as a tour guide for a company in Victoria. They did 21-day tours of the Arctic Circle and I was pumped for the new experiences. The program I would participate in had me in a passenger van with a cargo carrier on the top. Up to 20 Asian tourists explored Canada for their first time. I spent days organizing my backpack and training on the trails outside Nanaimo.

I made sure my health was as good as can be, I even decided that Hayden was my only son, and to have any more children wouldn't be fair to him. I missed him so much that I just couldn't see myself spending time with another child while not having my son by my side. I decided to get a vasectomy at the age of 35. This is my life, I figure, and I knew my limitations to love again. I would never have another opportunity for a child. This broke me deeply considering it was the only thing I ever wanted when I was younger and it kills me that Hayden is going through this now. I never wanted my son to be without a mother or a father.

With four days to go before I was set to leave for the Yukon with my new career, I was excited to finally try a new challenge and discover more of who I was and just how capable I was. As I was getting my gear together, lacing up my boots and heading out for a warm up hike with my backpack, the phone rang.

"Hey bro, how goes it? What are you up to today?" Tomas was calling from Prince George.

"Hey, I am just heading out for a hike. I leave in a few days," I said. I felt he had something to say to me.

"It's Mom again, bro, she is not well. Her neighbour called me last night and the police were there. She needs to get back into the hospital right away, can you go? I would but I am super busy with work up here, bro" he said.

"Really? Fuck!! Shit!! Bro I am heading to a new employer, new beginning, and in just few days," I replied, trying to maintain my attitude over the phone.

I quickly realized I needed to do this for our mother. For my brother and his family as well because he has a lot more at stake than I did at that point. "Yeah bro, I will head to Vancouver in the morning, I guess. I have to quit this new job even before I start."

I hung up the phone, raised my hands to the sky and yelled at the top of my voice. "Why? Why? Why me? What is it that I have done or am not doing that life throws so many curve balls at me and I continue to strike out?"

I drowned my thoughts with a bottle of rum. The next morning, I travelled to East Vancouver to find my mother.

It was another tour of duty that lasted several days, was somewhat overwhelming with emotions. There were periods similar to hiding in a jungle awaiting the enemy and fearing for your life. Except it was my mother's life and the enemy is her thoughts and actions that prompt response from the local authorities. Not too many days had gone by and she was back in the hospital. Fearing for her safety, she was restrained in a bed until the drugs kicked in. Neither my brother nor I could stand to see our mother in restraints. It was not something a kid should see, right? But, as time went by, situations repeated themselves and certain things became less shocking.

On the evening of November 26, 2006, driving home from work the rain was pounding. The rain had been fierce since the morning when I drove to work and it was steady throughout the day.

"C'mon wipers don't fail me now," I was telling them as I had to flip the switch to the faster wipe mode.

The rain was pounding the windshield so hard I had to turn the sound up on the radio in order to hear the music. I was working in Langford installing a sewer line for the municipality and living in Nanaimo. The drive was over an hour one way and with the torrential rains, you can double that time.

"Ah, another red light! C'mon man," I said as I drove through Duncan. Just as my car cames to a stop at the intersection, the rain falling in buckets with my wipers on high mode, my cell phone rang.

"Hello!" I answer. Tomas is on the other end.

"Hey bro, I have to tell you something."

All of a sudden, WHAM!!

"What the fuck!" I yelled as I am instantly pushed out of my seat against the seatbelt and into the steering wheel. "I've just been rear-ended, bro!" I said, but I could hear in his voice that what he had to say was much more dramatic than my traffic accident.

"Oh man. Mom is dead," he murmurs.

I asked him to repeat what he just said as I unbuckled myself and opened my door. Cell phone still at my ear, I heard Tomas crying on the other end. He said she had a heart attack and died instantly without any pain. I was in shock, both with this news as well as the car accident and the absolute rain fest coming down.

My mother had been living much better and for a longer period of time, mainly because of her relationship with another man. He was half her size, a short, skinny little man who had a huge heart. Willy spent eleven out of twenty years in prison for killing his wife's lover after he caught them in bed together. You would never think this guy had it in him but I guess he lost his shit and they wrestled. Well, he did his time and met our mother at a volunteer community work program. They were both involved with the Salvation Army. He took care of her as much he could and kept us brothers in the loop of her well being. They were together for few years and they really became good friends who looked out for one another.

Her death was extremely hard for Willy because they were holding hands walking down the street after having breakfast together. She apparently let go of Willy's hand and just as he looked over, her eyes closed. Reaching out for his best friend's arm, he realized something was wrong with her. Everything happened so fast and ferociously that she felt no pain and was quietly laying on the ground. Willy fell on top of her in shear agony and dismay. Reaching out for her, holding her face he prayed to God.

"Pray my love, wake up," he said, looking for something to happen.

The following few weeks, Tomas and Milan looked after our mother's affairs. This was hard on everyone and each had their own way of coping. I coped the way I knew: booze and drugs and some more booze. Returning to the Island, I felt so lost and abandoned—utterly alone. Over the next several months I moved from one place to another because nothing ever felt like home and keeping a job was a juggling act. I had to go through my second bankruptcy when my ex-wife decided to take me to court again, which becomes yet another low for me. It was becoming even more difficult to cope with. I was seeing Hayden as much as I possibly could and making each visit the best ever. As much as life's lows seemed to be constantly challenging I felt that things would always get better as long as I put the effort in.

Chapter 11 – Things Start to Click

In the next few years following 2007, I moved from Nanaimo to Shawnigan Lake where I had more space, even though it was more isolated down a dead end road. But, I was working steady as a foreman for a local excavation company and going to rehearsals at dinner theatre in the evenings. I lived on a property that was in poor condition, and previous tenants used a portion of the property for dumping garbage. I cleaned all that up over a period of weeks. I repainted inside and outside of the home, and made many repairs throughout the home. I loved doing it though, I started to think I should have my own property. Maybe one day.

Acting is where I needed to be, on stage or in front of the camera. Being part of the cast on a project was by far the most rewarding feeling I have ever encountered. Meeting with the regular film crews as a background performer, I was quickly becoming familiar on set. I learned the lingo, the rules and the expectations of an extra compared to "The Talent." Reminded me of my times working in the ditches as a labourer looking up at a backhoe operator thinking to myself, *One day! I will be in that seat.* It's the same as the ladder climb up in this new industry. *One day! I will be an actor,* I told myself.

Over the next few years I took any role that was presented to me. Zombie, monk homosexual, crossdresser, and after several projects I was consistently being called in for cop detective, fireman, anything with a uniform or suit roles. Auditions were plentiful whether it was on the Island or in Vancouver, which was frequently. Slowly I was landing small speaking roles, the odd commercial and eventually I was thirsty for more. I figured if I truly wanted to be an actor then this was where I felt in my heart that I belonged. I auditioned for the stage. Doing live acting in front of the audience was the best experience, I thought. Before long, I embraced this wonderful feeling when the audience would stand and applaud. Over the next dozen years and more I participated in just as many theatre productions. Everything from pantomime to musicals, Shakespeare, comedies and dramatic roles, and eventually I made it to principle roles as well.

Acting is my salvation, saved me from depression and gave me new direction and hope. I am meant to be a character actor, with the physical comedy that lets me explore myself without the barriers or stigma of my big stature. Also, through this whole journey I want to show my son that anything is possible for anyone who strives to try new things and challenges themselves to the fullest. As much as I wanted to become the father I had grown up dreaming of becoming, my opportunities were very limited and I hoped that somehow if Hayden saw me on the television or on stage that I would make an impression on him. And perhaps he would be proud of me. I knew my responsibilities though and it was to him.

As much as I wanted to become a great actor, I also had my support payments to his mother to pay. I would constantly give up on acting roles in order to work operating heavy equipment for the constant paychecks in order to get myself back on track. But, I could do theatre! Rehearsals were always in the evenings and shows on weekends, so I continued with that even though it never paid a penny. It was the opportunity to constantly do something that I enjoyed doing. You like playing tennis, then you go play on weekends or whenever you can, right? So, for me it is a downer when I can't audition or even do theatre when I am in the construction industry. Especially these days while I work away in camps.

But, even with the construction industry I strived to become the best I could. I have been part of 30 years in the heavy excavation industry in British Columbia and the biggest projects in history here. I look back now and take pride in the accomplishments that I achieved operating excavators and as foreman for some of the most talented people on the west coast. I have also strived for the experience in a project and I saw a lot of our province in the deepest isolated areas to downtown Vancouver. I wanted to achieve the most from the industry and I feel fortunate that I have had the opportunities along with my acting career. But between the two, I feel way more alive when I am surrounded by a cast during a production and it doesn't matter if its theatre or film. Everyone feels the same, the vibe is addictive. I finally feel like I've achieved some sort of greatness and inspiration. On the other hand, some experiences were deeper to my soul.

One such case was meeting a distressed young girl by the name of Amanda Todd on Highway 1 in Burnaby while on shift at work. She was on the evening news almost every night. She was bullied by some guy in Sweden over a long period of time and it was driving her to suicide attempts.

We were driving east on the highway doing our rounds checking pumps and generators on the huge Port Mann/Highway 1 project with the Kiewit Construction Company.

"Hey Henry, there are several cars parked in our work zone," said Jim to me as we drove closer.

"Let's pull over and see what's going on" I replied. I walked up to one of the vehicles parked and with my hard hat, vest and company truck a person quickly gets out and tells me that they almost hit a young girl.

"She just jumped out in front of me, I swerved to miss her," a gentleman tells me. "She ran off the highway and into the bushes here somewhere but it is getting dark and we cannot see very well. We'd like to know she is OK," another person from a second car said.

I grabbed a flashlight and Jim and I walked into the bushes. After not too long searching, we found a cute young girl of about 15 years old crouching with her hoodie hiding her face.

"Hey! Are you OK? We are here to help you," I said.

Almost immediately I heard police sirens. Almost two weeks later I heard her name on the news.

"Poor girl, what a shame," I said to Jim. "She killed herself this time,"

This really hit me in my heart; I really felt for her and wished I could have done more for her that night we found her. I would have liked to have said more, told her I cared.

Working on this big project and soaking in all the experience, I was known as the guy who got shit done. I worked day shift for over a year. My opportunities for auditions were slim but when I was put on night shift for two years, I took advantage of it all. I was doing auditions during the days—a couple a day sometimes—and not sleeping for more than 24 hours at times. Deep down I knew I was going to become a paid actor or host a travel show like Anthony Bourdain had. But, after a few years the biggest project in BC was coming to an end and I was once again in search of a new company to work for. My auditions slowed down again because working construction in the days does not leave much room to head downtown. I was not sure how people could continue with auditions and the price of housing these days. But, I don't give up. Sometimes I had to put auditions off to the side but eventually I knew I'd have other opportunities.

My next opportunities were good experiences for me. The next biggest project in the province was for hydro transmission towers. I was 1 of 6 operators chosen for a helicopter excavation crew. The pilot would drop each of us off at points on a mountain range where we'd individually excavate for the footings of the huge towers. This exceeded my expectations in this industry and I embraced all this adventure in my job and transferred it into my actor persona when the opportunity opened. I worked on that project for over 18 months till my good friend, Duane—friends since we were 15 years old—helped me with my next job opportunity. I worked in an open pit gravel mine for the next 3.5 years. Then I did deep excavation for tall buildings right downtown Vancouver, then up to northern Alberta in the oil sands industry, and then a hydro substation on the next biggest project in BC, the hydro dam. I was with Canadian and American companies for the time being but my next opportunity will be working internationally. Why not?

During my time back to the lower mainland I found myself reuniting with my old high school mates. This brought me great joy and I felt I was finally home. I saw friends I had not seen since Deanna and I left BC after she graduated in 1988. When my friends came to see me on stage or called me to say that they saw me on television one night was very rewarding. It was reminiscent of growing up with people who knew me from a past I tried to forget felt OK to me. But, I was not the young lost soul they once knew.

Looking back on the last year, 2018, I'm just holding my head up and wondering how I get through sometimes. How do others cope? Am I doing what is right for me? Why does it seem like I need to face these challenges constantly? Why don't I care what I do, where I am or where I'm going? What am I searching for? I have so many questions.

I would like to know where my son is and how he is doing. I'm waiting for his call one day, or a message that he is OK. I tried looking him up, and sent messages but never a reply. He is mad at me and I just have to wait. Hopefully one day my phone will ring and it is him. But, I truly feel I am tested by God. I am here to help others, and my reason for being on this planet is much greater than all this. I just wonder when I find this out. Seems I have been going through the motions and challenges since I was a kid. That it is my punishment for the lack of love in my life, a hug. Start by removing my father, then my mother, then my first love, then my wife and son, and now my brothers?

I am sitting at the table back at my brother's place. Here I feel loved.

"Hey bro, you hear back from anyone yet?" Tomas says, pouring a glass of red wine.

"No not yet, pour me one, too," I reply to him.

"Well what about that guy you bumped into a couple weeks back? I thought he said he would call you?" Tomas is leaning back in his chair while sipping at his glass.

One sunny day I was walking to the gym at the local recreation centre in Maple Ridge and I was wearing a worn out green MASH t-shirt. I was stopped by some older, gray-haired short man who was part of a group standing off to the side. A production company was in the gazeebo in the centre of town and they were in the middle of some film project. I had no clue, but I admit I was salivating as I walked through dreaming of an opportunity and reminiscing of my past experiences on set. So, this older gentlemen steps out in front of me and says, "Hey, excuse me, but don't I know you from somewhere?"

"I am not sure, I don't think so?" I quiclly answer back.

The fella scratches his head and looks at me, "Yeah, I never forget a face you know."

I put my backpack down on the sidewalk still startled. "Well, actually sir, I am an actor. Perhaps you saw my commercial or something? I was in an NFL and Kaltire commercial recently. I am not part of your production but I am available."

At this point another younger man walks over and says, "Excuse me Mr. Mel Damske, we are set and ready."

"Do you have any information on yourself? I have to get going now," he says to me.

I nod as I open my backpack and grab some papers. "Actually sir, I have a headshot and a resume if you are interested?"

He takes my information and shakes my hand telling me I have a good look about me and that he will pass my information to Jackie, his casting director. "Someone will you call you, Henry, very soon. I will get you something." He motions to me as he walks to his chair.

"Thank you sir, very much. I look forward to seeing you again, thank you!" I repeatedly say to him as I am on Cloud Nine.

Finally, I think, *I am the right person at the right time.* A few weeks go by and I don't hear anything.

In August 2018, my father back in Ontario is not doing too well. I decide to fly out to see him. He's had a long fight with Parkinson's Disease and now the onset of Dementia is making him weak in his age. I visited for a few weeks and made sure he and his wife, Shirley, were alright. In the meantime, I had no phone calls from Jackie the casting director. By now I had come to the realization that shit doesn't happen to me so I need to make things happen—my own adventure. I was in no rush to get anywhere and decided to take the train across Canada. Everyone should do it once at least, right? Toronto to Vancouver for 4 days and 4 nights should be interesting. I strive for adventure and exploring new places and perhaps along my journey I will meet my destiny? For whatever reason, deep down I am a hopeless romantic with a desire to feel loved. Until then, I continue to put one foot in front of the other, one day at a time, in search of new chapters in my life. Sometimes you just don't realize exactly what you need to make yourself happy but a long train ride helps! It turned out to be quite an adventure and I'm glad I went.

By December 2018, I would complete a job in northern Alberta. It was a short project but a highly adventurous one that I would embrace and make some good money. I would go from -40 to +40 in a few days. I operated and work with the biggest equipment in the world, and in extreme conditions. Then I took my first vacation in several years and travelled to Mexico by myself for ten days just before Christmas. I went by bus through Mexico and I was getting to know the people. I never stayed in a resort but experienced the local culture and stayed with my friend, Legna, who I met 20 years earlier on my way to Australia. We have always kept in touch and it is nice to have someone familiar with the language and culture.

I can't help but constantly feel that I am searching, that there is still something missing from my life. This last year I have become comfortable with who I am and not too concerned about the future. I know I can always earn some sort of income to get by. And with the sky rocketing rental prices I just have not made a decision where I want to live. I am counting on my life going in the right direction at the right time. For now, it is just me wandering the planet hopeful that the right opportunity presents itself. Whether I am in Prague, Vancouver, Victoria, Australia, Boston, Toronto—wherever I may end up as long as I feel loved, I don't mind.

In May 2019, I took a trip to Prague, Czech Republic for my cousin's wedding and to find the roots of my nationality. This has opened me up even more than I ever could have imagined. Going back to where your parents came from and connecting with that culture and language, foods and people is most welcoming. I look forward to returning and who knows, maybe I will stay for a while?

Nothing compares to Victoria though, one of the most beautiful cities in the world. It is where I come to visit my very good longtime friends, Phil, Chris and Sue. I feel a lot of the things I do nowadays is mostly a bonus. That by my age I have experienced a lot and I will be content if it all stopped now. But, till that day comes everything is a bonus.

Just be true to yourself and don't give up. Keep trying new things and make the best decisions for yourself. At age 49 I realize more of who I am and everything that has brought me to this point in my life. My advice is to travel and see the world, meet new people and eat different foods. Try new cultures, see and feel the life around you. Live.

Back at the dinner table. "How about the audition you went for? Are they supposed to call you?" Tomas asks me as he passes over the plate of moose roast that he shot and his wife cooked.

"Yes, my third callback, bro, they should be calling soon but I have an opportunity as a foreman now with a huge American company to work for as well, someone should call," I tell him while I check my cell.

I truly hoped a call would happen and not just another let down.

"Just stay positive, Henry. Good things do happen to those who never give up. I have a good feeling, brother," he says to me.

I figure, why not me? Just then my cell phone rings and I open the line.

"Hello?" I don't recognize the female voice on the other end.

"Henry Bartak? Can you hold a second? Someone would like to speak to you."

My hands start sweating and my mouth is dry. "Hello, I am doing well, thanks. I look forward to seeing you, thank you," I say, looking at Tomas with a huge smile on my face.

The End.

CPSIA information can be obtained
at www.ICGtesting.com
Printed in the USA
BVHW042045171220
594989BV00008B/19